Sew Gifts
with Love

Nancy Zieman

Published by

krause publications
An F&W Publications Company

700 East State Street • Iola, WI 54990-0001
715-445-2214 • 888-457-2873
www.krause.com

Please call or write for our free catalog of publications. Our toll-free number to place an order or obtain a free catalog is 800-258-0929 or please use our regular business telephone, 715-445-2214.

Library of Congress Catalog Number: 2003105294

ISBN: 0-87349-691-4

Printed in the United States of America

The following company or product names appear in this book:
Amazing Designer Series™ Hearts for All Seasons Memory Card, Amazing Designs® Lettering Pro™, Amazing Designs® The Amazing Box™, Amazing Designs® The Mini Amazing Box™, AppliqEase™ Lite, Avalon® by Madeira, Baby Lock® Ellageo, Binding and Hem Clips, Bubble Jet Rinse®, Bubble Jet Set 2000®, Clear Away, Colorfast Printer Fabric™, Dritz® Spray Adhesive, Dry Cover-Up™, Ezy-Hem® Gauge, Filmoplast Stic, Firm Hold, Fray Check™, Kleer-Fuse™, Hydro-Solve, Hydro-Stick Cut-Away, Little Foot®, Little Wooden Iron, Madeira Bobbinfil, Madeira Smooth Metallic Embroidery Thread, Madeira Textured Metallic Embroidery Thread, Mega Stay, Microtex Sharp Needles, Minute Miter, Patchwork Foot, Pattern Paper, Pellon® Sof-Stitch™, Pellon® Stitch-N-Tear®, Quick Bias, S-dSV™, SIA™, Sensuede™, Sewer's Fix-it Tape, Sewing With Nancy®, Sheer Stay, Amazing Designs® Size Express™, Suede 21, Softgrip® Scallop Shears, Sulky® Cut-Away Soft 'n Sheer™, Sulky® Totally Stable™, Sulky® Ultra Solvy™, Teflon Foot™, Templar®, Ultra Tear, Ultrasuede®, Wash-A-Way Wonder Tape, WashAway™ Foundation Paper

How many Nancys does it take to create a book?

Well, in this case, the answer is seven. More specifically, it's the seven of us pictured here. It doesn't quite take a village to write a book, but it does take a group effort from what I call "The Collective Nancy." After all, there is no "I" in Nancy!

This book began as a series of long brainstorming meetings, which then gave way to a flurry of activity in the sewing room, which resulted in the exquisite projects featured in this book.

Darlene May, the fabric buyer, continually searched for amazing treasures that she cleverly placed in the sewing room where the designers could not miss them. Her eye for color and taste for unique textures and patterns kept us all on the edges of our seats.

Donna Fenske and Kate Bashynski, project designers, transformed those fabrics into beautiful gifts. On any given day, you could walk into the sewing room and notice a twinkle in Kate or Donna's eye, and return later to be rewarded with yet another masterpiece.

Amy Stalp, the writer, then wrote the instructions for the projects, as well as the inspiring titles and descriptions. Her enthusiasm for finding the perfect title for each project was unwavering. That spirit is reflected in her words and sets the tone of the book.

Laure Noe, the illustrator, added the visual component of the book, creating detailed illustrations for the projects and setting up the breathtaking photos. Walking into the photo room when Laure was setting up photos was like entering another, more magical world.

The Collective Nancy:
Back row, from left: Amy Stalp, Laure Noe, Nancy Zieman
Middle row: Pat Hahn, Donna Fenske
Front row: Darlene May, Kate Bashynski
Not pictured: Dale Hall

Dale Hall, the photograher, then captured that world exquisitely on film. His stunning photos truly make this book a work of art.

Pat Hahn, the editor, lent her keen eye for accuracy to the pages, making sure that every "i" was dotted and every "t" was crossed.

From fabric selection to project creation to writing to illustrating to the final edit, the author of this book is truly "The Collective Nancy."

We hope you enjoy creating these gifts as much as we enjoyed creating the book.

Nancy Zieman

Contents

CHAPTER 1

Paper-Pieced Presents

Nancy sewed a little quilt,
Its pieces all in line.
And everyone who saw it said,
I wish that it were mine!

When you give someone a paper-pieced gift, the first reaction might be amazement at the tiny pieces so accurately pieced together. But no one needs to know that you didn't spend hours slaving away over templates and traditional patchwork techniques. (That can be our little secret!)

In this chapter, use paper piecing to create elegant and comforting gifts. From exquisite silk purses to a soothing eye pillow, these gifts are sure to make anyone's day special. And only you need to know that creating them was a "piece" of cake!

Paper Piecing Basics

Paper piecing is an alternate approach to quilting. Extremely accurate, it's ideal for detailed designs, making it simple to join sections of small projects. Instead of precisely cutting each part of a design and meticulously joining sections with exact ¼" seams, piece designs by machine stitching them onto a paper foundation. It's as easy as paint-by-number!

Start with a basic design such as the pineapple, page 138 or the heart, page 139. Then enlarge it, reduce it, use several designs in one project – the possibilities are endless! In this chapter, master the basics by paper piecing two designs; then use those designs to create a variety of projects just by changing the size and using different fabrics.

Tools

❦ *Paper* – Use a lightweight see-through paper such as Pattern Paper for the foundation for the design. Or use tissue paper. Another possibility: With washable fabrics, use WashAway Foundation Paper to make it easy to remove the paper after stitching is completed. WashAway quickly dissolves in water, so in 10 seconds flat, your completed project can be paper-free. Trace designs onto this paper or print them directly onto the paper with a photocopier or computer printer.

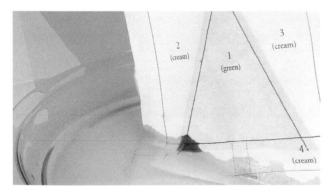

❦ *18mm rotary cutter* – Designed for intricate and detailed cutting, this rotary cutter is perfect for trimming away seam allowances from the small sections in paper-pieced designs.

❦ *Little Wooden Iron* – Use this tool to press each section after stitching.

- 🌹 *Small rotary cutting mat and ruler* – Position a small cutting mat next to your machine. Use it with a 1" x 6" ruler or a 4" square ruler and rotary cutter to accurately cut small sections of your paper-pieced design right next to your machine.

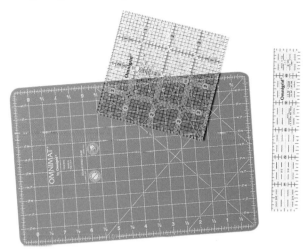

- 🌹 *Stiletto (or "That Purple Thang")* – These tools aid in removing the paper foundation from your pieced design after stitching.

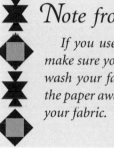

Fabrics

Almost any type of fabric can be used for paper piecing. When you are just beginning, it's best to use a tightly woven fabric. As you become more proficient, experiment with specialty fabrics like silk. Because these fabrics tend to slip more than wovens such as cottons, it's best to have some experience before using them.

If you select a printed fabric, be aware that only a small portion of that print will be visible in the completed project. Avoid choosing a fabric that has a definite pattern. Because paper-pieced sections are often very small, you rarely see that pattern in the finished design.

Note from Nancy

If you use WashAway Foundation Paper, make sure your fabric is washable. Then prewash your fabric. Otherwise, when washing the paper away, you could get water marks on your fabric.

Paper Piecing a Pineapple Design

Setting Up the Machine

1. Adjust the sewing machine for a straight stitch with a stitch length of 1.5 (15 to 18 stitches per inch). The short stitch length is very durable and makes it easy to tear away the paper sections after all the stitching is completed.
2. Use the standard sewing machine presser foot or an open toe foot. The open toe foot provides excellent visibility, so you can more easily see where you are stitching.
3. Use a universal needle.
4. Thread both the top and bobbin of the machine with all-purpose thread.

Preparing the Pattern

1. Trace or photocopy the pineapple design, page 138, onto paper. If tracing, also transfer the numbers to indicate the sequence in which sections are joined.

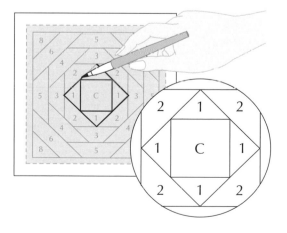

2. Add positioning lines to each section of the pattern.
- Align the ¼" mark on a 1" x 6" ruler with one of the pattern's stitching lines.
- Crease the paper along the ruler's edge. Repeat for all the stitching lines.

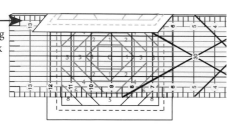

Match stitching line to ¼" mark on ruler; fold paper along ruler edge

 **Note from Nancy**

This step may seem unusual, yet it's a great timesaver. This crease aids in positioning fabric on the wrong side of the pattern and in trimming seam allowances. Folding the paper back after stitching provides a built-in guideline for trimming the fabric.

Cutting Fabrics for the Pineapple Blocks

1. Strip widths will vary with each project. Measure the width of each section of the design. A strip must always be at least as wide as the widest section that uses that fabric, plus ¾" to 1" for seam allowances.

2. Select two coordinating fabrics. For each block:
- Cut two 1½" wide strips from Fabrics A and B.
- Cut a 2" Fabric A center square.

3. *Note: For different size blocks, adjust the strip widths as follows:*
- Pin, page 16: Cut one 1½" wide strip from Fabrics A and B and a 1½" Fabric A center square.
- Tote, page 17: Cut two 3" wide strips from Fabrics A and B and a 3" Fabric A center square.

Paper Piecing the Pineapple Blocks

1. Place all fabrics on the nonprinted side of the paper, with right sides together.

2. Piece the design, starting with the center square.
- Place the Fabric A square over the center section of the design. Pin it in place from the printed side of the paper.

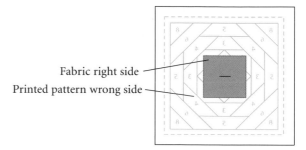

Fabric right side

Printed pattern wrong side

- Meet a Fabric B strip along the crease line between the center fabric square and one section 1, with right sides together. Finger pin the fabrics together.

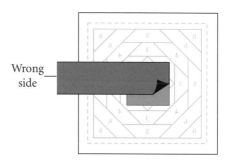

Wrong side

 **Note from Nancy**

You could also pin the strip to the center square, but I find it saves time and is much more efficient to simply finger pin the two fabrics together.

- From the printed side of the paper, stitch along the line joining the two sections, starting and ending a stitch or two beyond the line.

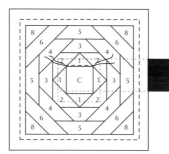

Stitch from paper side

- Trim the thread tails close to the paper. This keeps the back of the fabric neat and avoids having a mass of threads when the project is completed.
- Fold the paper back along the crease line to expose the seam allowance. Trim the seam along the crease using a rotary cutter, mat, and ruler. Trim only the seam allowance, not the paper.

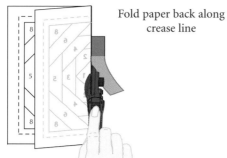

Fold paper back along crease line

• Press the joined section so it covers the seam and the portion of the design numbered "1." Finger press the seam or use the Little Wooden Iron or a traditional iron on a no-steam setting.

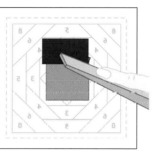

Press joined section to cover seam

• Move to the next #1 section. Align the Fabric B strip along the trimmed cut edge of the center strip with right sides together. Finger pin the fabrics together.

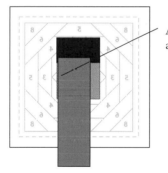

Align Fabric B along cut edge

• Stitch from the printed side, again starting and stopping a few stitches beyond the line. Trim and press the seam.

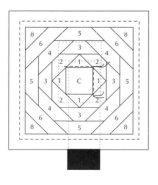

Stitch from paper side

• Repeat for the remaining #1 sections.

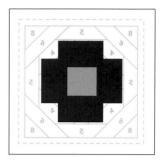

3. After completing all the #1 sections, change to Fabric A and stitch all the #2 sections, using the same technique.

4. Finish the full and partial pineapple blocks using the same technique, joining the sections in numerical sequence. Use Fabric A for all even-numbered sections and Fabric B for all odd-numbered sections.

5. *Optional*: Tear away the paper from the wrong side of the fabric.

Note from Nancy

I prefer to leave the paper attached until after I join the blocks. The paper backing provides a precise marked stitching line so you can accurately join sections. After stitching is completed, the needle perforations make it easy to remove the paper from the back of the pieced sections.

This striking black and gold purse will add a dramatic touch to any evening ensemble. It's simple to create, so you can easily make one for every well-accessorized woman on your list! Use purchased cording for the strap or create your own. Add beaded embellishments to complete the purse, for an extravagant-looking gift sure to attract many midnight admirers.

Moonlight Melody Purse

Materials Needed   Finished size: approximately 4½" x 8"

- Pineapple blocks (full and partial):
  - ¼ yd. Fabric A (center square and even-numbered sections)
  - ⅛ yd. Fabric B (odd-numbered sections)
- Lining: ¼ yd. Fabric B
- Cording: 1½ yd. purchased cording (or make custom cording using your favorite technique)
- Strap carriers: scraps of synthetic suede, ribbon, or trim
- *Optional*: beads for embellishment

Making the Purse

1. Piece and join the full and partial blocks.
   - Piece two each of the full and partial pineapple blocks as detailed on pages 9-11.
   - Trim each section along the marked dotted cutting lines, using a rotary cutter, ruler, and mat.

- Join the longest edge of the partial block to a corresponding side of the full block, with right sides together.

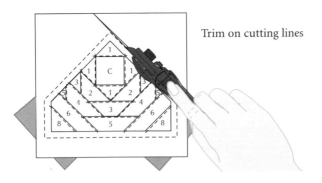

Trim on cutting lines

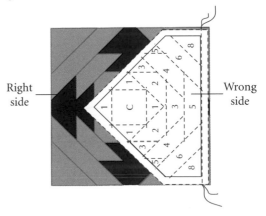

Right side   Wrong side

- Repeat with the remaining full and partial blocks.
2. Create a lining pattern by folding under the seam allowance of the partial block and matching it to the stitching line of the full block.

Fold under seam allowance ▼

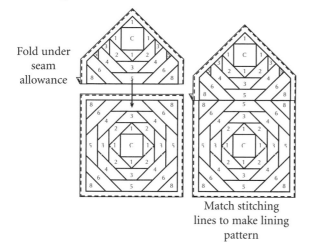

Match stitching lines to make lining pattern

3. Cut the lining sections and strap carriers to complete the purse.
   - Cut two lining sections using the lining pattern.
   - Cut two strap carriers from synthetic suede, ribbon, or trim. Cut each piece about ¼" to ½" x 1", depending on the strap size.
   - Cut a piece of cording for the strap approximately 50" to 54" long or the desired length.
4. Meet the shorter edges of the carriers; position and pin the carriers to each side of one of the pieced purse sections, 1" down from the top edge.

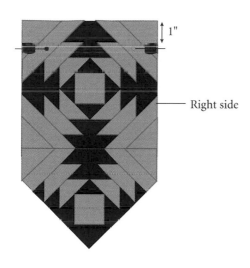

1"

Right side

5. Join the two purse sections, with right sides together.
   - Stitch the side and lower edges of the purse together, leaving the top open.

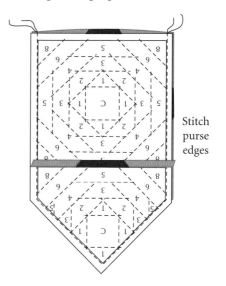

Stitch purse edges

- Remove the paper. Turn the purse right side out.
6. Repeat, meeting and stitching the lining sections.
7. Join the purse and the lining.
   - Pin and stitch the lining to the purse at the upper edge, with right sides together, matching the seams and leaving an opening for turning.

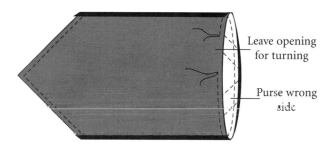

Leave opening for turning

Purse wrong side

- Turn the purse right side out. Stitch the opening closed.
8. Thread the cording through the strap carrier. To securely hold the strap in place, stitch next to the cording, creating a smaller opening in the carrier.
9. *Optional*: Sew beads on the purse and a beaded tassel at the tip.

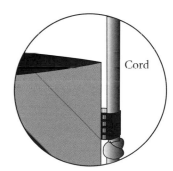

Cord

Like the notes in a symphony, the elements of this evening bag blend together in wonderful harmony. Silky smooth fabrics reflect light, creating a radiant glow. "Audition" different fabrics to find the perfect combination for you or a friend. This evening bag is so simple, you'll have plenty of time to make one to match every outfit in your friend's closet as well as your own, and still make it to the concert on time!

Symphony of Silk Evening Bag

Materials Needed   Finished size: approximately 5½" x 5½"

- Pineapple blocks (full and partial):
  - ⅛ yd. Fabric A (center squares and even-numbered sections)
  - ⅛ yd. Fabric B (odd-numbered sections)
- Front panel and gusset: ¼ yd. Fabric A

- Lining and gusset: ¼ yd. Fabric B
- Cording: 1½ yd. purchased cording (or make custom cording using your favorite technique)
- *Optional*: beads for embellishment

Making the Evening Bag

1. Piece and join the full and partial blocks.
   - Piece one full and one partial pineapple block as detailed on pages 9-11.
   - Join the blocks as detailed for the Moonlight Melody Purse, pages 12-13.

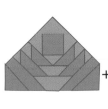

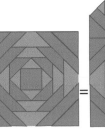

2. Cut fabrics to complete the evening bag.
   - Fabric A:
     - Cut one piece the size of the full block.
     - Cut one gusset, using the pattern on page 138.

Fabric A

- Fabric B (lining):
  - Cut one piece the size of the pieced blocks (full and partial block joined).
  - Cut one piece the size of the full block.
  - Cut one gusset.

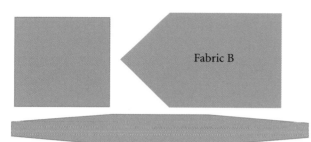

Fabric B

- Cut a piece of cording for the strap, approximately 50" to 54" long or the desired length.

Note from Nancy

As another option, feature the pieced block on the front of the evening bag. Then join the partial block to the solid Fabric A block. Or piece two full blocks for the front and back of the evening bag.

3. Stitch one gusset to the pieced blocks.
   - Mark the center of the Fabric A gusset. Mark the center of the lower edge of the pieced block and the Fabric A full block.
   - Meet the Fabric A gusset to the pieced block, with right sides together, matching the center marks. Pin the gusset in place, working around the sides and the lower edge.
   - Stitch from the lower edge to the top edge, clipping and pivoting at the corners.

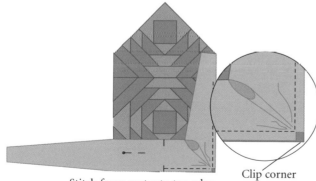

Stitch from center to top edge   Clip corner

4. Pin and stitch the Fabric A full block to the gusset section, with right sides together, following the same procedure. Turn the evening bag right side out.
5. Join the Fabric B lining pieces, with right sides together, following the same process.
6. Pin or baste the shoulder cord or strap to the upper edge of the gusset on the right side of the evening bag, meeting the cut edges. If desired, add decorative beads and/or yarns at the tip of the flap, again meeting the cut edges.
7. Meet the right sides of the lining and the evening bag. Stitch, clipping the corner at the pivot point near the flap seam and leaving an opening for turning.
8. Turn the evening bag right side out. Stitch the opening closed.
9. *Optional:* Add beaded embellishments to the evening bag flap. Here are some helpful hints for adding beaded accents.
   - Use a very fine beading needle. Standard sewing needles are too big to fit through the holes in small beads.
   - For best results, use cotton thread coated with beeswax, or a silk thread.
   - Use several different shapes and colors of beads to enhance the fabric.
   - To create fringe, knot string around the last bead, then string as many beads as desired before stitching it to your project.
   - To create a tassel, knot several strings together around one bead. Thread the beads onto each string and knot the string around the last bead. Then knot all the strings together and stitch the tassel in place.

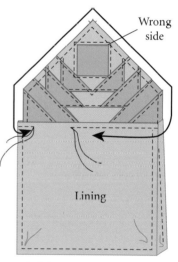

Baste straps and optional decoration

Wrong side

Lining

Stitch lining to purse, leaving an opening to turn

If you're on pins and needles trying to decide on gifts for your friends and family, calm your nerves and make lovely pins for them instead. To create these small wonders, we reduced the pineapple design used for the purse and the evening bag. When you start making these pins, you'll see that good things really do come in small packages!

Poetry in Motion Pins

Materials Needed Finished size: approximately 2¼" x 2¼"

- Scraps of Fabrics A and B
- Scraps of nonraveling fabric such as felt or synthetic suede
- Card stock
- Pin back
- *Optional:* beads for embellishment

Making the Pins

1. Piece one pineapple block as detailed on pages 9-11, using the reduced pineapple pattern, page 138. Be sure to allow a generous 1" seam allowance at the outer edges. It's not necessary to remove the paper from the back of the design.

2. Cut a piece of card stock the finished size of the pin. If necessary, use several layers to provide sufficient sta-

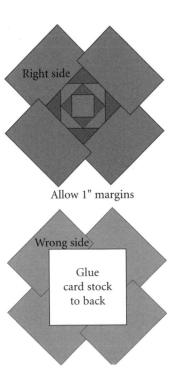

Right side

Allow 1" margins

Wrong side

Glue card stock to back

bility. Glue the card stock to the wrong side of the pieced block.

3. Glue the seam allowances to the back of the pieced block. If necessary, trim the seam allowances to reduce bulk.

4. Cut a piece of nonraveling fabric (for example, felt or synthetic suede) slightly smaller than the size of the finished pin.

5. Cut two small holes in the nonraveling fabric to accommodate the pin back. Insert the pin.

6. Glue the backing to the pin.

7. *Optional:* Sew on beads for embellishment.

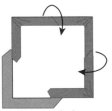

Trim and glue seam allowances

Attach backing and pin

Whether you're toting around books, crafting projects, makeup, or your daily planner, you'll look sleek and stylish when you carry this elegant tote. Construct the front and back by paper piecing pineapple blocks, then add a handle, and voila – you have a luxurious gift sure to complement anyone's wardrobe!

Tonal Splendor Tote

Materials Needed   Finished size: approximately 15½" x 15½" x 3½"

- Pineapple blocks:
  - ⅔ yd. Fabric A (center square and even-numbered sections)
  - ½ yd. Fabric B (odd-numbered sections)
- Lining: ½ yd. Fabric B

- Handle and side/base strips:
  - ⅜ yd. Fabric A
  - ⅜ yd. Fabric B
- Fusible interfacing: ⅛ yd.

Making the Tote

1. Piece the pineapple blocks.
   - Using a photocopier, enlarge the pineapple block pattern, page 138, by 155%.
   - Paper piece eight blocks as detailed on pages 9-11.
   - Create the tote front by joining four blocks as shown. Repeat for the tote back.
2. Cut fabrics to complete the tote.
   - Cut two 16" Fabric B squares for the tote lining.
   - Cut two 4" wide crosswise strips from both Fabrics A and B for the side/base strips.
   - Join the Fabric A strips, with rights sides together, on the diagonal to avoid bulk. Repeat with the Fabric B strips.

3. Assemble the tote.
- Mark ¼" from the cut edges at all corners of the tote front with a fabric marking pen or chalk.
- Use the edge of the presser foot as a stitching guide to ensure accurate ¼" seams.
- Position one end of the side/base strip along the right edge of the tote front, with right sides together, extending the strip approximately ½" above the front.

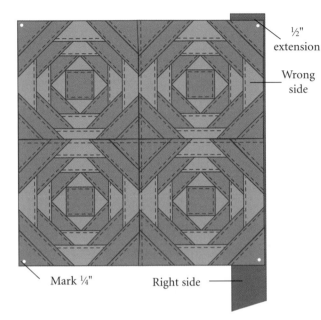

½" extension

Wrong side

Mark ¼"   Right side

- With the edges aligned, place the side/base strip next to the machine bed and begin stitching at the upper ¼" mark. Stitch to the lower ¼" mark, stopping with the needle down in the fabric. Backstitch to reinforce the stitching.

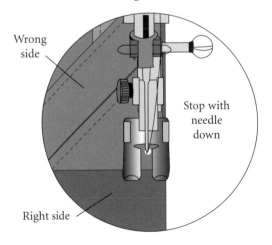

Wrong side

Stop with needle down

Right side

- Raise the presser foot and remove the fabric from the machine. Nip the side/base strip perpendicular to the ¼" mark, almost to the seamline.

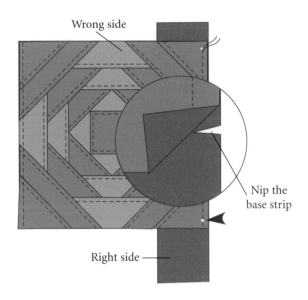

Wrong side

Nip the base strip

Right side

- Pivot the tote front. Reposition the needle at the ¼" mark, aligning the lower edge of the tote with the side/base strip. Backstitch. Stitch to the next ¼" mark. Backstitch.

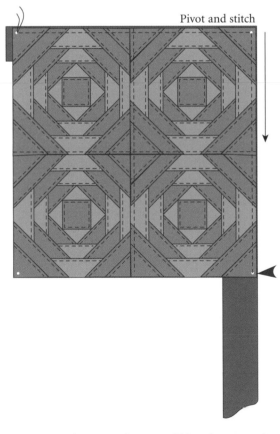

Pivot and stitch

- Repeat at the second corner. Trim the excess length from the side/base strip, leaving a ½" extension.

- Attach the tote back to the remaining edge of the side/base strip.

4. Assemble the tote lining in the same manner as the tote.

5. Finish the tote bag.
- Slip the tote bag into the lining, with right sides together, matching the seams and aligning the top edges.
- Stitch across the top edge of the front and back at least ¼" from the cut edges, leaving the sides open to attach the handle.

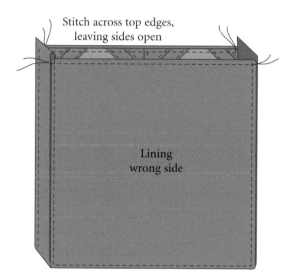

Stitch across top edges, leaving sides open

Lining
wrong side

- Turn the tote right side out through the handle holes.

6. Attach the handles.
- Cut one 4" wide crosswise strip from both Fabrics A and B, approximately 33" long or the desired length.
- Cut two strips of fusible interfacing the same size as the handle strips.
- Position the interfacing on the wrong sides of the handle strips. Press to fuse.
- Meet the handle strips, right sides together, meeting the raw edges. Stitch along both lengthwise edges.

Interfacing

- Turn the handle right side out. Press.
- Meet the ends of the handle to the tote, with right sides together, making sure to keep the lining free.

- Stitch the handle to the tote.

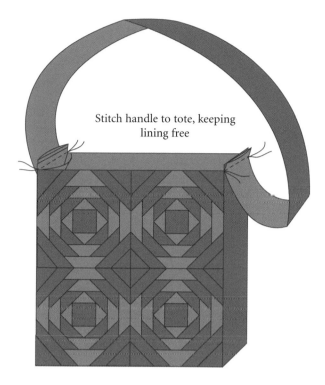

Stitch handle to tote, keeping lining free

- Turn under and press the raw edges on the lining. Hand stitch the lining to the handle.

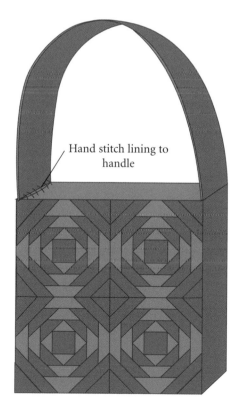

Hand stitch lining to handle

Use this mended heart design to create gifts that come straight from the heart. Instead of cutting strips, use templates to create this paper-pieced design. If you know someone who is in serious need of pampering, then the following projects are just what you need to show how much you really care!

Paper Piecing a Heart Design

Preparing the Pattern

1. Trace or photocopy the number of copies needed for your project, plus two additional copies, using the pattern on page 139. If tracing the design, transfer the hash marks and numbers.

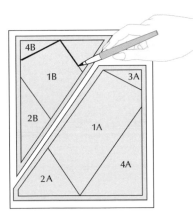

Trace outline, numbers, and hash marks

2. Add creased positioning lines to the number of copies needed for stitching the blocks, as detailed on page 10.

3. Use the remaining two copies to streamline piecing.
   - Pin fabric swatches to the nonprinted side of one copy to identify the colorations for each section.
   - Use the second copy to make "patterns" for the various sections of the design.
     - Mark the front of each pattern section: "Cut [# needed for project], this side facing up."
     - Cut out each shape in the design.

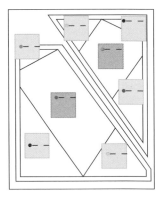

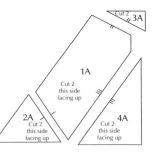

Cutting Fabrics for the Heart Blocks

1. Cut starter strips for the paper piecing.
   - Measure the widest area for each pattern piece. Add a generous 1" to that dimension to determine the size of the starter strip.

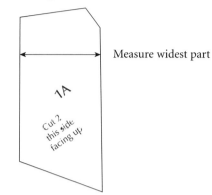

Measure widest part

   - Cut starter strips for each pattern section. Place all the fabric layers right sides down (wrong sides up).
   - Place each shape on the determined fabric color, with the pattern printed side facing up. If several strips of a coloration are needed to cut the required number of shapes, save time by stacking the strips, with right sides down, and cutting multiples at the same time.

2. Roughly cut out each shape, allowing generous ¼" seam allowances. It's not necessary to measure precisely; simply allow ¼" or more at each edge of the pattern. Cut the number needed of each section.
3. Separate the cut fabrics for each half block so they don't accidentally get mixed together.

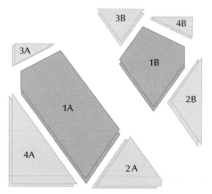

Paper Piecing the Heart Blocks

1. Paper piece the first half of the heart.
   - Place fabric section 1A behind the corresponding area on the paper pattern, with the wrong side of the fabric meeting the unprinted side of the paper. Pin the fabric in place from the printed side of the paper.

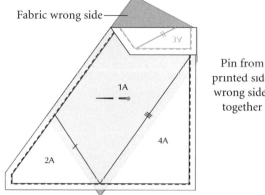

Fabric wrong side

Pin from printed side, wrong sides together

   - Meet the edge of fabric section 2A marked with a single hash mark to the 1A edge, with right sides together. Finger pin the fabrics together.

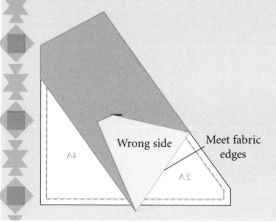

Note from Nancy

You could also pin these sections together, but it saves time and is more efficient to simply finger pin. You may want to double check the positioning by pinning along the stitching line before stitching. Then fold the fabric in place to ensure it completely covers the pattern area.

Wrong side

Meet fabric edges

- From the printed side of the paper, stitch along the line joining the two sections, starting and ending two or three stitches beyond the line.

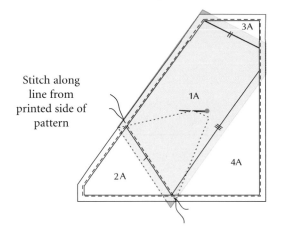

Stitch along line from printed side of pattern

- Repeat the process for each of the remaining heart half blocks. Repeating the same step on each block is an easy way to speed and simplify production of several identical pieces.
- Trim the thread tails close to the paper. This keeps the back of the fabric neat and avoids a mass of threads when the project is completed.
- Fold the paper back along the creased line. Trim the seam allowance along the crease using a rotary cutter, mat, and ruler.

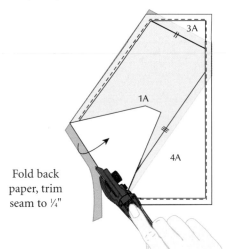

Fold back paper, trim seam to ¼"

- Press the joined section so it covers the seam and the portion of the design numbered 2A. Finger press the seam, or use the Little Wooden Iron or a traditional iron on a no-steam setting. Again, repeat this step for each block. Pin the center of the section in place to ensure it does not move.

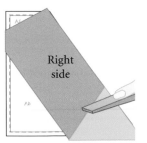

Right side

- Meet the edge of fabric section 3A marked with a double hash mark to the edge of 1A, with right sides together. Finger pin the fabrics together; check the positioning. Then stitch from the printed side, again starting and stopping a few stitches beyond the line. Press and trim the seam.
- Repeat for each block.
- Repeat the process to add fabric section 4A.
- Trim the block to the finished size.

2. Use the same process to paper piece the second halves of the hearts, using sections 1B, 2B, 3B, and 4B.

3. Stitch the opposite pieced heart halves together, aligning the intersection of the two halves to form the lower right edge of the heart.

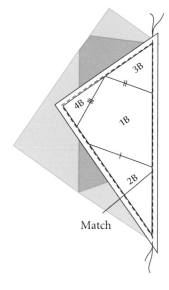

Match

- Pin or finger pin and stitch the sections together, following the stitching line on the paper pattern to form the [# needed] heart blocks.
- Press each block with a dry iron.
- Trim the block to the finished size, allowing ¼" seam allowances on all edges.

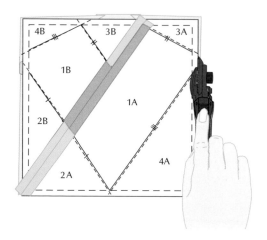

- Do not remove the paper backing until the blocks are joined. The paper backing provides a precise marked stitching line so you can accurately join the sections. After the stitching is completed, the needle perforations make it easy to remove the paper from the back of the pieced sections.

Stitch a gift that lets everyone know your heart is in the right place. Piece six heart blocks and add them to a simple pillowcase. The construction is easy, and you can experiment with different fabric combinations to accent any décor. Whether this pillowcase is used for a full night of beauty sleep, or a 20-minute catnap, it's sure to chase worries away and bring plenty of sweet dreams.

Sweet Dreams Pillowcase

Materials Needed Finished size: approximately 21" x 35"

- Pieced heart blocks:
  - ³⁄₈ yd. Fabric A (sections 1A and 1B)
  - ⁵⁄₈ yd. Fabric B (sections 2A, 3A, 4A, 2B, 3B, and 4B)
- Pillowcase:
  - ⁷⁄₈ yd. Fabric C (main section)
  - ³⁄₈ yd. Fabric D (accent and border)

Making the Pillowcase

1. Cut out the pillowcase sections.
- Fabric C: Cut one 28" x 42½" rectangle.
- Fabric D:
  - Cut one 2" x 42½" strip (accent strip).
  - Cut one 9" x 42½" rectangle (border strip).

2. Construct the main section of the pillowcase.
- Fold the Fabric C rectangle, with right sides together, meeting the 28" edges. Stitch the seam, using a ¼" seam allowance.

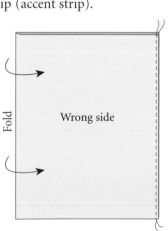

- Press the seam flat; zigzag or serge the edges together.
- Fold the seam toward the center of the pillowcase along the stitching line, wrapping the corner. Begin stitching at the fold and sew one end of the pillowcase closed. Press the seam flat; zigzag or serge the edges together.

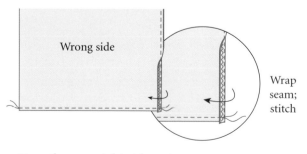

- Turn the case right side out.

3. Create the pieced heart cuff for the pillowcase.
- Piece six heart blocks as detailed on pages 20-22.
- Sew the heart blocks into a tube.
  - Meet two heart blocks, with right sides together, rotating one block 180°. Carefully pin along the stitching line on the foundation paper.
  - Stitch along the stitching line.

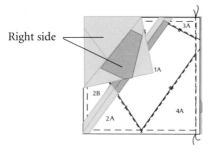

Right side

- Repeat, adding each heart block, rotating every other one until all six blocks are joined.

- Meet the two end blocks, with right sides together. Stitch along the stitching line.

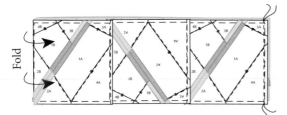

Fold

- Seam the 9" x 42½" Fabric D border strip, with right sides together, meeting the short edges. Press the seam open. Turn the strip right side out.
- Slip the heart block tube over the border tube, with the right sides together. Stitch, following the stitching lines of the foundation paper. Press the seam flat; then open.

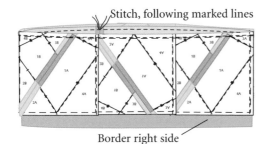

Stitch, following marked lines

Border right side

- Remove the foundation paper from the pieced heart blocks.

- Fold the border in half, with wrong sides together, meeting the cut edges. Press.

Fold border in half

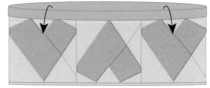

4. Attach the border and accent strip to the pillowcase.
- Seam the Fabric D accent strip, with right sides together, meeting the short edges. Press the seam open.
- Fold the accent strip in half, with wrong sides together, meeting the cut edges. Press.
- Machine baste the accent tube to the right side of the border, meeting the cut edges and matching the seamlines.

Baste accent tube to border

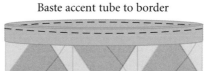

- Slip the border over the pillowcase, with the accent tube next to the right side of Fabric C, matching the seamlines. Stitch the seam.

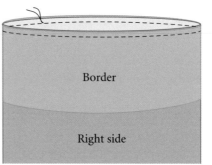

Border

Right side

- Serge or zigzag the edges. Press the seam toward the border.

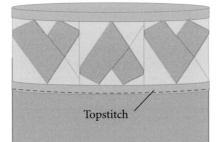

Topstitch

- Press the accent band away from the pieced heart border.
- *Optional:* Topstitch the accent band close to the fold.

If you feel like you're carrying the weight of the world on your shoulders – or have someone on your gift list who is – then stitch this comforting neck roll to soothe the tension away. Fill it with rice, buckwheat hulls, or cherry pits, and heat it in the microwave to provide warmth and relief. When you give this neck roll to your friends and family, they'll never give you the cold shoulder again!

Color Me Comforted Neck Roll

Materials Needed   Finished size: approximately 7" x 35"

- Pieced heart blocks:
  - ⅛ yd. Fabric A (sections 1A and 1B)
  - ⅛ yd. Fabric B (sections 2A, 3A, 4A, 2B, 3B, and 4B)

- Neck roll:
  - ½ yd. Fabric B
  - ¼ yd. Fabric C
  - Cotton batting: two 8" x 9" rectangles
  - Paper-backed fusible web

Making the Neck Roll

1. Make a pattern for the neck roll.
- Cut an 8" x 18" rectangle of Pattern Paper.
- Fold the paper in half, meeting the lengthwise edges.
- Place the 45° line of a quilting ruler along the fold, starting at one end. Mark along the edge of the ruler; cut along the traced line.
- Open the paper pattern. Write "Place on fold" along the straight short end of the pattern.

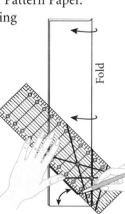

2. Fold Fabric B, meeting the selvages. Place the pattern on the fabric, aligning the fold lines. Cut two.

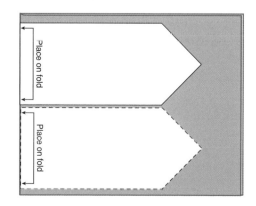

3. Piece the heart blocks.
- Reduce the heart design pattern, page 139, by 50%.
- Piece two heart blocks as detailed on pages 20-22.
- If the blocks are pieced on WashAway Foundation Paper, it is not necessary to remove it at this time. The paper is soft enough to leave in the project, and it will dissolve when the project is washed. If another foundation paper is used, remove it before adding the pieced blocks to the fabric base.

4. Add the pieced heart blocks to both ends of one of the Fabric B sections.
- Prepare the Fabric C framing squares.
  - Trace two 5½" squares onto the paper side of the paper-backed fusible web.

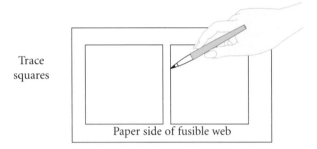

Trace squares

Paper side of fusible web

  - Roughly cut out the traced squares.
  - Press the fusible web to the wrong side of Fabric C. Let the fabric cool.

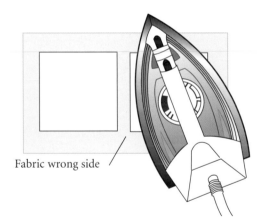

Fabric wrong side

  - Cut out the squares, following the outlines. Peel off the paper backing.

Remove paper backing

- Position the frames on point on opposite ends of one of the neck roll pieces, 1½" from the diagonal edges. Fuse in place.

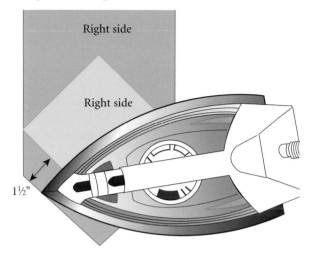

Right side

Right side

1½"

- Satin stitch the square in place.
  - Set the machine for a narrow zigzag, about 2.0 to 3.0 width.
  - Insert a machine embroidery needle.
  - Thread the top of the machine with embroidery thread and use a lightweight thread such as Madeira Bobbinfil or cotton prewound bobbins in the bobbin.
  - Replace the machine's standard presser foot with an open toe foot. The opening in the front of the foot lets you see precisely where you're stitching and a groove on the underside provides room for the stitches to easily pass under the foot.
  - Back the fabric with a tear-away stabilizer.
  - Satin stitch around the square.

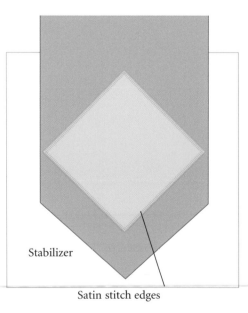

Stabilizer

Satin stitch edges

- Spray the wrong side of the pieced heart block with adhesive fabric spray, such as Dritz Spray Adhesive.
- Position the pieced heart blocks over the frame squares, placing the block 3½" above the tip and 1½" from the sides, as shown.
- Satin stitch around the pieced heart blocks.

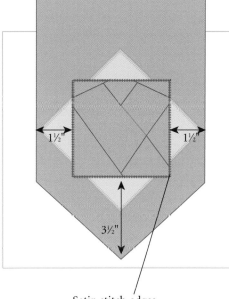

Satin stitch edges

5. Construct the neck roll.
- Meet the fabric sections, with right sides together. Place a piece of cotton batting at each end of the neck roll; trim to fit the neck roll.
- Stitch a ¼" seam along one edge of the neck roll. Trim the batting close to the stitching line. Press the seam flat; then fold it along the stitching line toward the center of the neck roll.

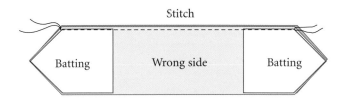

- Stitch the adjacent edge of the neck roll, beginning at the fold and sewing to the next edge. (This is a wrapped corner.) Trim the batting and press the seam as for the first edge.

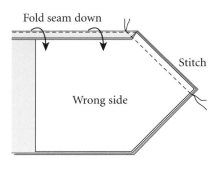

- Repeat, wrapping the corners on the remaining sides, leaving a 4" to 5" opening along the final lengthwise edge.

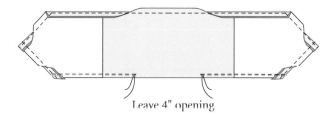

- Turn the neck roll right side out. Press.
- Straight stitch through all the layers around the outer edge of the satin stitched squares, extending the stitching to the edges of the neck roll at the sides as shown.

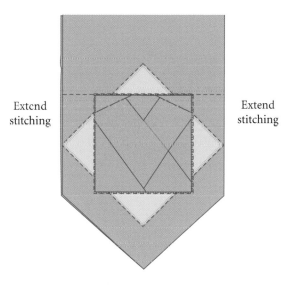

- Fill the neck roll with two pounds of rice, buckwheat hulls, or cherry pits. Stitch the opening closed.
6. To use the neck roll, heat it in the microwave for two minutes. Move the filling inside the neck roll from side to side to distribute the heat; then place the neck roll on your body wherever you want soothing heat.

Wear your heart on your sleeve – or on your face! This soft, eye soothing pillow is the perfect way to relax after a long, stressful day. Fill the eye-catching pillow with hot or cold inserts and let your worries melt away. Or wear the pillow while traveling in a car, train, or airplane to guarantee an uninterrupted nap!

Easy on the Eyes Soothing Pillow

Materials Needed   Finished size: approximately 5½" x 8½"

- Pieced heart blocks:
  - ⅛ yd. Fabric A (sections 1A and 1B)
  - ⅛ yd. Fabric B (sections 2A, 3A, 4A, 2B, 3B, and 4B)
- Eye soothing pillow:
  - ¼ yd. Fabric C (sashing and framing)
  - Cotton batting: two 7" x 10" rectangles

Making the Pillow

1. Prepare the heart design pattern.
   - Reduce the original design, page 139, by 50%. (If you've made the neck roll, use that pattern.)
   - Reduce the 50% design by 64%.
   - Add ¼" seam allowances to the pattern.
   (*Note*: When the pattern is reduced, the seam allowances are also reduced. Therefore, you need to redraw the seam allowances to equal ¼".)

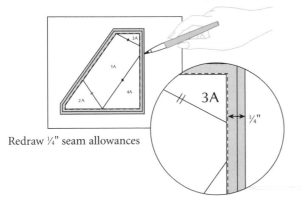

Redraw ¼" seam allowances

2. Piece two heart blocks as detailed on pages 20-22.

3. Assemble the pillow top.
   - Cut the fabrics.
     - Cut one 1¼" x 3½" Fabric C sashing strip.
     - Cut one 2" wide Fabric C crosswise strip. Subcut this into four 2" x 7" rectangles (framing strips).
   - Meet the sashing strip to the right edge of one heart block, with right sides together. Stitch from the printed side of the paper, sewing along the marked seamline.
   - Repeat, adding the second heart block to the sashing strip. Press the seams toward the sashing strip.
   - Meet the framing strips to the top and bottom edges of the

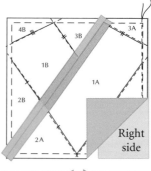

pieced heart blocks, with right sides together. Stitch from the printed side of the paper, sewing along the marked seamline.
- Repeat, adding framing strips to the left and right edges of the pieced heart blocks.

- Trace or photocopy the half pattern, page 142, onto Pattern Paper and cut it out along the outside lines.
- Fold the pillow top in half, with wrong sides together, meeting the short edges.
- Position the pattern along the fold line, centering the heart design. Trace the pattern on the pillow top.
- Cut out the pillow top. Cut out a piece of batting using the same pattern piece. Position the wrong side of the pillow top over the batting; pin or machine baste close to the outer edge.

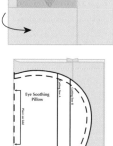

4. Create the pillow backing.
- Prepare the pattern.
  - Cut two 7" x 10" rectangles of Pattern Paper. Fold, meeting the 7" edges.
  - Position the pattern along the fold. Trace and cut out two patterns. Mark "Cutting Line A" on one pattern and "Cutting Line B" on the second pattern.
  - Cut one pattern along Cutting Line A and the second along Cutting Line B.
  - Cut one of each pattern piece from Fabric C.

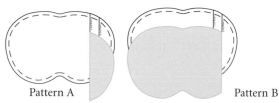

Pattern A   Pattern B

- Cut Pattern B from batting.

- Turn under the straight edge of the Pattern A section ¼"; press. Turn under another ¼"; press. Stitch the hem in place.
- Meet the batting to the wrong side of the Pattern B section. Trim ¼" from the straight edge of the batting to reduce bulk.
- Turn under the straight edge of the Pattern B section ¼"; do not catch the batting; press. Turn under another ¼", this time catching the batting. Stitch the hem, making sure to catch the batting in the stitching. Pin or machine baste close to the outer edge.

Batting

5. Construct the pillow.
- Place the pillow top right side up.
- Place the Pattern B section, with the right side down, over the pillow top. The two fabric sections should now be right sides together.

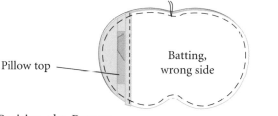

Pillow top   Batting, wrong side

- Position the Pattern A section, with the wrong side up, on the backing as shown.
- Pin the layers together.
- Stitch around the pillow, using a ¼" seam.
- Trim the seam allowances with a pinking shears to reduce bulk.
- Turn the pillow right side out.
- *Optional:* Attach a thin elastic strap to the pillow so it stays in place when you're not lying down.

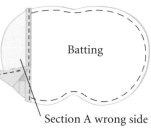

Batting

Section A wrong side

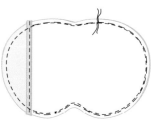

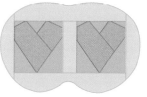

6. Insert a hot pack, cold pack, or soothing gel pack into the flap. Or skip the insert and enjoy the softness of the batting. Then sit back, relax, and enjoy some well-deserved pampering!

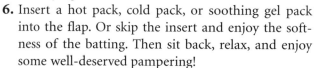

CHAPTER 2

Punched Suede Sensations

*Nancy had a piece of suede,
It felt so smooth and fine.
And when she punched it full of holes,
She made a neat design.*

If you hate the thought of shopping for gifts, then skip the mall and work out your frustration as you create gifts that pack a punch! Use leather punch tools to add complex designs to synthetic suede projects, then sit back and listen to the praise. Luxurious yet practical synthetic suede is an ideal fabric for creating unique gifts.

The projects featured in this chapter allow you to exercise your imagination and your upper body! Combine three different shapes of leather punch tools to create intricate designs on a variety of projects, from pillows to picture frames – even Christmas ornaments. When you experience this fabric, it's sure to be love at first sight – and touch!

Punched Suede Basics

Punching suede is a suprisingly easy way to make exquisite gifts. Simply choose a design, make a reusable template, punch holes in synthetic suede fabric, and enjoy the beautiful results. Starting with synthetic suede is half the battle. This super-soft fabric will soothe the spirits of even the roughest person on your gift list.

Use this technique with the designs in this book, then experiment with your own designs. Once you start, you'll see how changing combinations of the three shapes of leather punch tools will yield vastly different results. Punched suede is perfect for all kinds of projects – big and small – from delicate snowflake ornaments to bold home décor pillows.

Tools

❦ *Leather punch trio* (leather punch tools, rawhide mallet, and hardwood block) – Interchange the leaf, teardrop, and round shaped leather punch tools to create unique designs. When using the leather tools, be sure to work on a thick hardwood surface (for example, oak or maple rather than soft pine). A standard buttonhole cutter block is too small to withstand the hammering involved in leather punching. To do the punching, use a rawhide mallet, which absorbs shock and reduces noise.

❦ *Templar* – Use this lightweight plastic sheet to create reusable templates for easy and accurate cutting. Because it is heat resistant, an iron will not melt this durable material.

❦ *Small sharp fine pointed scissors* – Small scissors are ideal for trimming away extra fabric if the punch does not completely cut through the suede.

❦ *½" buttonhole punch* – Use this to create lacing holes in the suede.

❦ *Softgrip Scallop Shears* – These shears add a decorative finishing touch to fabrics that don't ravel, such as synthetic suede.

- 💗 *Air or water erasable fabric marking pen or pencil* – These tools work great for marking punch designs on synthetic suede.
- 💗 *Tapes* (such as Wash-A-Way Wonder Tape and Sewer's Fix-it Tape) – Pinning suede is difficult; these tapes temporarily hold suede layers together without damaging the surface.
- 💗 *Ball point bodkin* – Use this tool to thread laces through punched openings.

Fabric

All of the projects in this chapter were made using synthetic suede (for example, Suede 21, Sensuede, or Ultrasuede). Each has the luxurious look and drape, soft feel, and tough durability of natural suede yet offers sew-ability, stain and soil resistance, and easy care. These fabrics are completely machine washable and dryable, and wrinkle resistant. Because they don't ravel, edges can be easily finished with a scallop shears or rotary cutter. Their stain and abrasion resistance makes them practical for a variety of items, such as purses and pillows. The internal "scrim" allows the fabric to breathe and to remain strong and supple.

Setting Up the Machine

1. Insert a size 80 Microtex Sharp needle. This needle has a special point that more easily pierces the fabric and helps prevent skipped stitches.
2. Use a Teflon foot. The Teflon-coated foot glides over hard-to-sew fabrics such as synthetic suede, preventing the fabric from tugging and pulling against the foot.
3. Thread both the bobbin and the top of the machine with coordinating all-purpose thread.
4. Lengthen stitches to 8 to 10 stitches per inch, approximately a 3.5 setting.

Preparing the Template

1. Prepare templates of the designs using Templar.
   - Select a design. Use the designs on pages 140-142, or create a design of your own.
   - Trace the design onto Templar. Often the pattern will be repeated several times on the project, so you can use the template many times. If the pattern has a repeat, indicate it on the template using arrows.

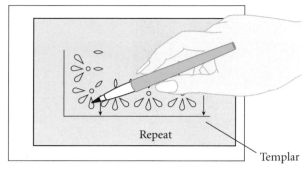

- Punch the design in the Templar using the leather punch tools.
  - Place the Templar over a hardwood block.
  - Use a mallet and punches to create the marked design.
2. Mark the design on the fabric.
   - Tape the template to the wrong side of the fabric. Trace the design using an air or water erasable fabric marking pen.

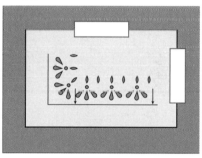

Tape template to wrong side of fabric

- Reposition the template as needed to mark the remainder of the design.

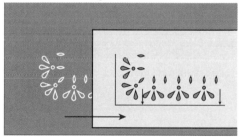

Reposition template to mark remainder of design

Punching the Design

- Place the synthetic suede over a hardwood block.
- Use a mallet and punches to create the design.
- If the punch does not completely cut through the suede, use a very sharp scissors to carefully snip the shape free.

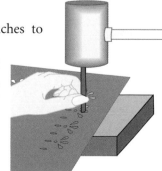

Decorate your tree this year with handmade charm and let it snow, let it snow, let it snow! These delicate-looking snowflakes are easy to make — you'll have a tree's worth in an afternoon! For a fun winter activity, make a steaming pot of hot chocolate, throw in lots of marshmallows, and invite some friends over for a snowflake-making party.

Each snowflake requires minimal fabric and looks great wherever you decide to hang it. No matter what the weather is doing outside, when you display these snowflakes, you won't have to settle for dreaming of a white Christmas; you'll have one in your home!

Let it Snow Snowflakes

Materials Needed	Finished size: small, approximately 2½" diameter; large, approximately 3½" diameter

- Small pieces of synthetic suede (5" square will yield one large and one small snowflake)
- Silver thread such as Madeira's Textured or Smooth Metallic Embroidery Thread
- Templar

Making the Snowflakes

1. Mark the pattern on a piece of synthetic suede.
   - Photocopy or trace the snowflake patterns, page 141, onto Templar.
   - Punch the snowflake designs in the Templar as detailed on page 33. Cut out each template, following the dotted lines around the outside of the snowflake.

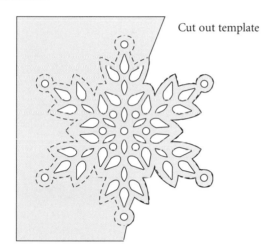

Cut out template

- Position the template over the wrong side of the fabric. Trace the design and the cutting line.

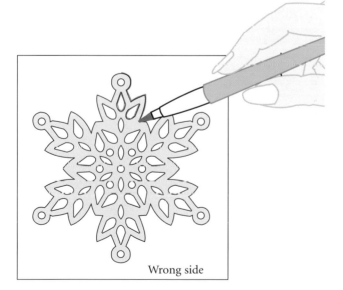

Wrong side

2. Punch the design as detailed on page 33.
3. Trim and hang the ornament.
   - Carefully cut around the outside of the punched design, following the marked cutting line.

- Cut a 9" length of silver thread. Knot the cut ends together.

- Pass the knotted end through an outer hole in the snowflake and bring the knotted end through the loop formed. Gently pull to secure the thread around the fabric.

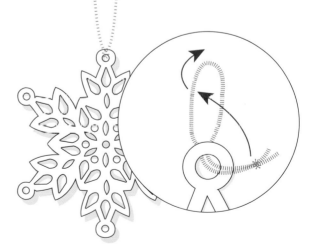

- Make more snowflakes and create a snow flurry for your holiday decorating and gifts.

Say cheese – and create an elegant gift to capture treasured memories. This exquisite punched suede picture frame slips easily over a clear acrylic frame, enhancing whatever photo you choose to display. Punch an intricate-looking design in one fabric, and choose a second color to peek through the holes. Large or small, this frame makes a great accent for any décor, and a special way to show off cherished photos.

Photo opening: approximately 5½" x 7½"

Pleased as Punch Picture Frame

Materials Needed
Finished size: large frame, approximately 9¾" x 11¾"; small frame, approximately 5¾" x 7¾"

- Water-soluble basting tape
- Templar
- Large frame:
  - Two 10" x 12" Fabric A rectangles
  - One 10" x 12" Fabric B rectangle
  - 8½" x 11" clear acrylic frame
- Small frame:
  - Two 6" x 8" Fabric A rectangles
  - One 6" x 8" Fabric B rectangle
  - 5" x 7" clear acrylic frame
- Softgrip Scallop Shears

Making the Frame

1. For the large frame, cut out the center of one 10" x 12" Fabric A rectangle. For the small frame, cut out the center of one 6" x 8" Fabric A rectangle.
- For the large frame, measure and mark 2¼" from all four sides. For the small frame, measure and mark 2" from the sides.
- Cut along the marked lines.

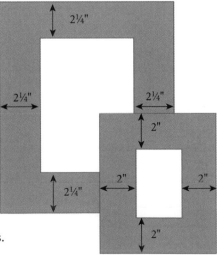

2. Transfer the design to the fabric.
- Trace the frame design, page 141, onto Templar and punch the design as detailed on page 33.
- Position the template over the wrong side of the Fabric A frame, aligning the interior corners with the marks on the template.

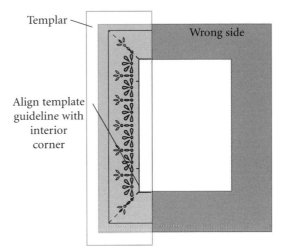

Templar

Wrong side

Align template guideline with interior corner

- Mark the design, repositioning the template for each side. For the small frame, mark the corners first. Then reposition the template and center the designs for each side.

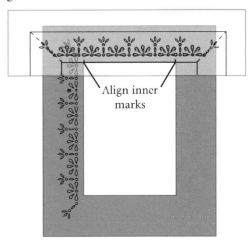

Align inner marks

3. Punch the design as detailed on page 33.
4. Construct the frame front.
   - Place the Fabric B rectangle on a flat surface with the right side up. Position the Fabric A frame over the Fabric B rectangle with the right side up. Secure the corners with small pieces of water-soluble basting tape.

Fabric B

Water-soluble basting tape

- Stitch around the interior opening, ¼" from the cut edges. Stitch across the lower edge, beginning and ending ¼" from the corners.
- Cut out the center ¼" from the stitching line. *Optional:* Use Scallop Shears to scallop the interior edges, being careful not to cut through the stitching.

Stitch around opening and across lower edge

5. Assemble the frame.
   - Position the punched frame front over the remaining Fabric A rectangle, with wrong sides together. If needed, secure the corners with small pieces of water-soluble basting tape.

Cut out center

- Stitch ¼" from the outer edges through all the layers of the three unstitched sides. *Optional:* Scallop the outer edges, being careful not to cut through the stitching.

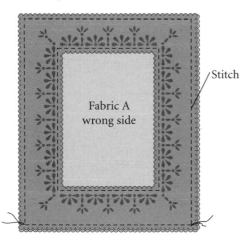

Fabric A wrong side

Stitch

6. Slip the suede frame over a clear acrylic frame and insert a photo. If necessary, tape the photo to the acrylic frame to keep it in place. *Optional:* Cut away a slight scoop from the lower edge of the frame back so it fits smoothly over the acrylic frame.

Spiced Sage Pillows

The Eyelet-Edged Pillow and the Patchwork Punch Pillow (page 40) look like they were plucked straight from the vine in a dense forest, lush with foliage. Their luxurious fabric and rich colors will add a truly elegant touch to any decorating scheme. Construction is simple – you can work out your frustration as you create the pillows! Look in your spice rack for color inspiration – cayenne pepper, cloves, cinnamon. The pillows will look just as delicious as they sound. Make several sets to coordinate with every room in your house, or make a set for a friend. These pillows are stunning gifts for any occasion!

Eyelet-Edged Pillow

The Eyelet-Edged Pillow features delicate punched edging and graceful lacing strips. Construction is refreshingly easy – no sewing machine required!

Materials Needed
Finished size: approximately 16" square

- Fabric A: one 17" square (pillow front)
- Fabric B:
  - One 17" square (pillow back)
  - Enough ¼" wide strips to equal 68" length (allow extra for joining strips if necessary)
- 16" pillow form
- Templar
- Water-soluble basting tape
- Softgrip Scallop Shears

Making the Pillow

1. Trace the eyelet design, page 140, onto Templar and punch the design as detailed on page 33.
2. Mark the fabrics.

- Using the template and a fabric marking pen or pencil, transfer all the markings onto the wrong side of the 17" Fabric A square.

- Mark the four corners first, aligning the corner guideline with the fabric corner.

- Using the repeat pattern, designated by arrows, mark the sides between the marked corners. Adjust the positions as needed to evenly space the designs.

• Punch the design as detailed on page 33.
• Position the Fabric A square over the Fabric B square, with wrong sides together, aligning the edges. Secure the corners with small pieces of water soluble basting tape.
• Using the punched Fabric A square as a guide, punch only the leaf shapes in the Fabric B square.

Fabric B
wrong side

3. Assemble the pillow.
   • "Sew" the layers together through the punched leaf openings with the Fabric B lacing strips, using a hand running stitch. If not in one continuous piece, leave the ends of each lacing strip loose and knot them together after sewing. Leave one side almost completely open for inserting the pillow form.

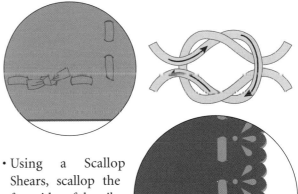

Note from Nancy

A ball point bodkin is a handy tool to use when lacing the layers together. Thread the laces through the bodkin's large eye to easily "sew" the pillow.

Sew layers together

   • Insert the pillow form.
   • Continue sewing the pillow shut, knotting the ends with a square knot on the Fabric B side of the pillow.

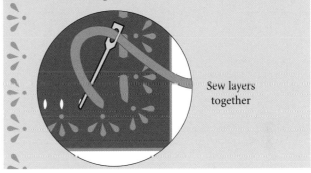

   • Using a Scallop Shears, scallop the four sides of the pillow, cutting both layers of the synthetic suede at the same time.

Note from Nancy

Scalloping edges is a finishing touch that should only be done after cutting with a regular scissors. Use the Scallop Shears to trim rather than cut for a beautifully finished edge.

This pillow features an intricately punched panel, which is "sewn" onto a pillow. Choose softer, muted colors in similar shades for an understated, elegant effect. Or make a more dramatic statement with three bold colors. Either way, use this pillow to express your true personality, whether you're quietly refined or a wild child at heart.

Patchwork Punch Pillow

Materials Needed | Finished size: approximately 18" square

- One 18" x 29" rectangle Fabric A
- One 8" x 16" rectangle Fabric B
- One 18" x 22" rectangle Fabric C
- 18" pillow form
- Templar
- Water-soluble basting tape
- Softgrip Scallop Shears

Making the Pillow

1. Cut the fabrics.
   - Fabric A:
     - Cut one 8" x 18" rectangle (pillow face).
     - Cut one 10½" x 18" rectangle (pillow back).
     - Cut two ⅛" x 27" strips (lacing strips).
   - Fabric B:
     - Cut one 7½" square (punched panel).
     - Cut five ½" x 8" strips (back ties).
   - Fabric C:
     - Cut one 10¾" x 18" rectangle (pillow face).
     - Cut one 10½" x 18" rectangle (pillow back).
2. Transfer the design to the fabric.
   - Trace the panel design, page 140, onto Templar and punch the design as detailed on page 33.
   - Trace the design onto the wrong side of the 7½" Fabric B square using a fabric marking pen or pencil.

- Punch the design as detailed on page 33.
- Using a Scallop Shears, scallop only three sides of the square.

Scallop three sides

3. Create the pillow face.
- Position the punched Fabric B panel over the right side of the 8" x 18" Fabric A rectangle, ½" from the side and bottom edges of the rectangle, aligning the straight edge of the panel with one 18" edge of the Fabric A rectangle.

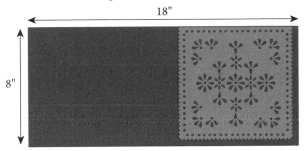

Position panel ½" from edges

- Using the Fabric B square as a guide, mark the lacing holes along the four sides of the panel and along one 18" edge of the Fabric A rectangle.
  - Mark the holes with the Fabric B square in its original position, then slide the Fabric B square to the left, matching the previous marks.
  - Return the Fabric B square to its original position.

- Punch the marked holes in the Fabric A rectangle.
- Using a running stitch and a Fabric A lacing strip, "scw" the Fabric B square to the Fabric A rectangle along the three scalloped sides. To secure the strip, knot each end on the wrong side of the fabric.

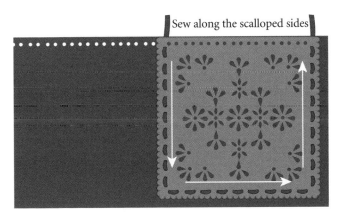

Sew along the scalloped sides

- Using a Scallop Shears, scallop the long edge of the Fabric A rectangle and the Fabric B panel, cutting both layers at the same time.

Scallop edge through both layers

- Position the wrong side of the Fabric A rectangle over the right side of the 10¾" x 18" Fabric C rectangle, overlapping the rectangles to measure 18" wide.

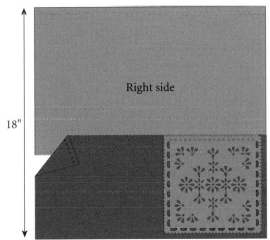

Right side

- Using the Fabric A rectangle as a guide, mark and punch lacing holes in the Fabric C rectangle.
- Sew the rectangles together with the Fabric A lacing strips, using a hand running stitch and a ball point bodkin.

4. Create the pillow back.
- Position the 10½" x 18" Fabric C rectangle over the 10½" x 18" Fabric A rectangle, overlapping the rectangles to measure 18" square. Tape the sections in place using small pieces of water-soluble basting tape.

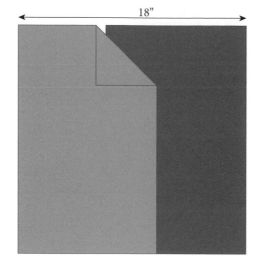

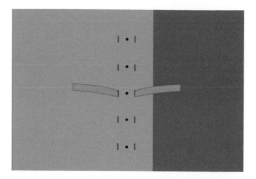

- Mark the pillow back and cut the lacing slits.
  - Mark a dot in the center of the square, 1" from the cut edge.
  - Mark two dots above and below the first dot, approximately 2" apart, for a total of five dots as shown.

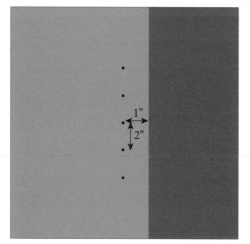

1"

2"

- Using a ½" buttonhole cutter, cut slits ½" to the left and right of each dot, cutting through both layers.

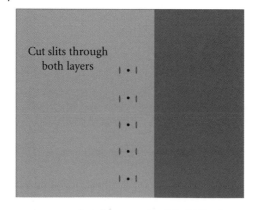

Cut slits through both layers

- Insert one of the ½" x 8" ties through the center set of slits to hold the back together.

5. Assemble the pillow.
- Meet the pillow face and back with right sides together. Stitch the outer edges, using ¼" seam allowances, catching the lacing strips in the seam.
  - Stitch one side seam from cut edge to cut edge.
  - Fold the seam along the stitching line, wrapping the seam allowances to one side.
  - Stitch the next side seam, beginning at the fold and stitching to the cut edge.

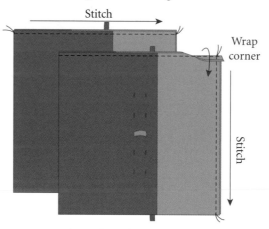

Stitch

Wrap corner

Stitch

- Wrap and stitch each corner in this manner.
- Remove the tie and tape pieces from the pillow back.
- Turn the pillow right side out and insert the 18" pillow form.
- Thread the ties through the slits on the pillow back, closing each with a square knot.

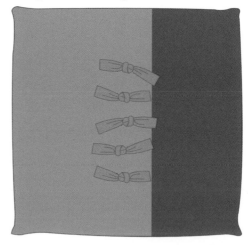

No formal ensemble is complete without a fabulous bag. The punched suede design on this evening bag will add a touch of class to any outfit. The contrasting lining fabric peeking through the punched design adds just the right amount of pizzazz. It's the perfect accessory for a night on the town.

Paint the Town Red Evening Bag

Materials Needed Finished size: approximately 7" x 8½"

- ⅓ yd. synthetic suede
- ¾ yd. lining fabric

- Templar

Making the Evening Bag

1. Make the pattern for the evening bag.
- Trace the flap half-pattern, page 142, including the positioning points and notches, onto Pattern Paper.
- Flip the paper over, align the center line, and trace the other half of the pattern. Cut out the pattern.
- Add 14" length to the flap pattern.

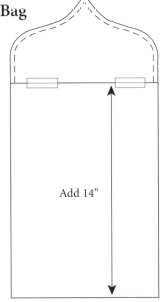

Add 14"

2. Cut out one evening bag from suede and two from lining fabric. Trim ⅛" from the short straight end of the linings. This helps prevent the lining from showing on the outside of the bag.

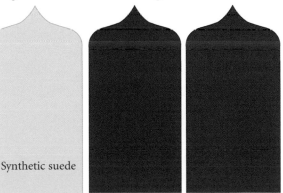

Synthetic suede

Trim ⅛" from bottom edge of lining

3. Transfer the design to the fabric.
- Trace the flap half-pattern onto Templar, marking the center line.

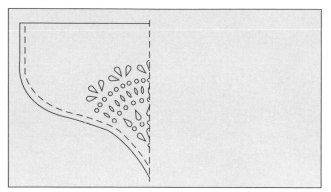

Trace half of design on Templar

- Flip the template over, align the center line, and trace the other half of the design.

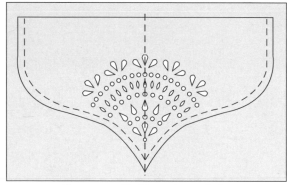

Trace second half; punch out design

- Punch the design as detailed on page 33.
- Fold the suede flap in half. Mark the center line on the wrong side.
- Position the template over the wrong side of the synthetic suede flap, aligning the center lines.
- Mark the design.

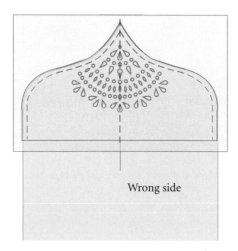

Wrong side

4. Punch the design as detailed on page 33.

5. Assemble the bag.
- Place the evening bag, with the right side down, on a flat surface. Position one lining section on top, with the right side down. Machine baste.

Lining wrong side

- Meet the second lining piece to the suede side of the evening bag, with right sides together. Stitch a ¼" seam along the curved flap edge, starting and ending at the notches. Also stitch along the opposite short edge.

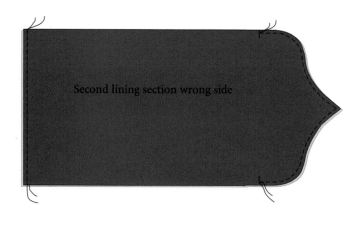

Second lining section wrong side

- Clip and notch the curved edge. Clip to the stitching line at the flap notch. Reinforce the stitching at the point.

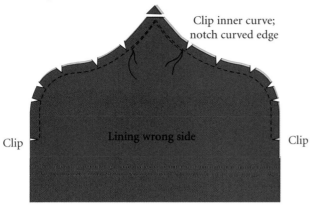

Clip inner curve; notch curved edge

Lining wrong side

Clip   Clip

- Press the seam on the short end toward the lining. Understitch the seam, stitching only the seam allowance to the lining.

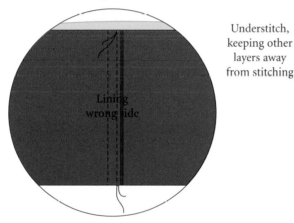

Understitch, keeping other layers away from stitching

Lining wrong side

- Turn the bag right side out. Press both stitched edges from the lining side to avoid damaging the suede surface.
- Stitch the side seams.
  - Meet the understitched edge to the flap notches, with right sides together, aligning the cut edges. Stitch the sides with ¼" seams.

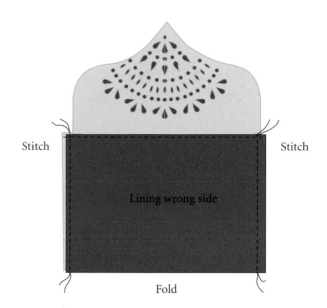

Stitch   Stitch

Lining wrong side

Fold

- Serge or zigzag the seams to prevent raveling.

- Miter the lower corners.
  - Fold the lower edges so the side seam is stacked on the top of the lower fold, forming a triangle.
  - Stitch perpendicular to the seam 1" from the point, reinforcing the stitching at each end.

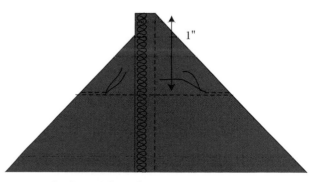

1"

- Turn the bag right side out.

CHAPTER 3

Strip Quilting Keepsakes

Nancy cut some fabric strips,
Arranged them in a row.
She quickly stitched them into quilts.
The process was not slow!

If you can cut strips; you can make great things happen! Strip quilting is a streamlined process for creating beautiful patchwork creations. With this technique, you won't have to cut tiny pieces and little squares — cvcrything starts with strips of fabric. Simply stitch them together to form stratas and create your quilt top – it's just that easy.

The projects featured in this chapter make great gifts for anyone on your list. Whether you're making a quilt to welcome a new baby into the world or need a cozy gift for a special man in your life, you'll find what you're looking for! From edges that fray to quilts for play, this chapter is sure to get you in the gift-giving mood!

Strip Quilting Basics

Strip quilting is a quick and efficient way to create complex-looking patterns. If you've been living with the misconception that quilting is a time-consuming activity that involves intricate processes, then open your mind to the simple technique of strip quilting. In this chapter, learn a fresh approach! Start by joining strips of fabric to form stratas. Then recut those strips and rejoin sections to create interesting blocks and designs.

Using this simplified technique, you can create a wide variety of projects, including a scarf, mittens, towels, cosmetic bags, and a clever jewelry tray. You can also use a variety of different seaming techniques, such as traditional, frayed-edge, serged flatlocked, and kissed seams, to create completely different looks. After working your way through this chapter, you'll see quilting in a whole new light!

Tools

- ❦ *Rotary cutter, mat, and ruler* – Use these tools for accurate cutting. Rotary cutters, mats, and rulers are available in a variety of sizes; choose tools that work for you.

- ❦ *Size 1 Curved Basting Pins* – Use these pins to baste quilt layers together. These nickel-plated brass pins won't rust, and they're the right angle for easy, comfortable insertion.

- ❦ *Binding and Hem Clips* – These rust-proof, nickel-plated steel clips hold binding firmly in place during stitching and are easy to remove with just a little flip.

- ❦ *Sewer's Fix-it Tape* – This tape is especially handy when working with fleece. Use it to temporarily baste fleece layers together. It removes easily without damaging the surface of the fabric or leaving a residue.

- ❦ *Little Foot or Patchwork Foot* – These specialty quilting presser feet are the precise width needed for accurate ¼" seams.

- ❦ *Stiletto* – Use this handy tool to guide fabric under the presser foot and to prevent seams from shifting and puckering.

Cutting and Seaming

1. Prewash and press the fabrics. **Note:** *If using fleece, skip this step.*
2. Cut the fabrics for the quilt.
   - Use rotary cutting techniques.
     - Meet the fabric selvages. Hold the fabric by the selvages and allow it to drop in front of you. Fabric may not be perfectly straight as it comes from the bolt. If you see diagonal wrinkles, shift the fabric along one of the selvages until it falls perfectly straight. (Cut edges may be uneven.)

Meet selvages

Shift selvages until fabric falls straight

Fabric does not fall straight

   - Place the fabric on a cutting mat, with the fold away from you. Align the fold with one of the horizontal lines on the cutting mat.
   - Meet the selvage edges to the center fold, aligning all the edges.

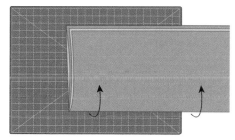
Fold again, meeting selvages to first fold

The fabric is now folded in four layers. If you're right handed, place the majority of the fabric to your right. If you're left handed, place the majority of the fabric to your left.
     - Straighten the fabric edge by aligning a quilting ruler with the markings on the mat. Stabilize the ruler with one hand and use a rotary cutter to cut along the edge of the ruler.

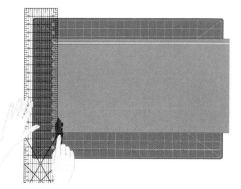

   - Cut the strips using a sharp rotary cutter, aligning the cut edge of the fabric with the marks on the ruler at the needed strip width.

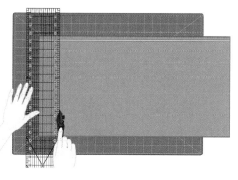

3. Stitch the strips together, creating a strata.
   - Set up the sewing machine or serger as directed for your chosen seaming technique.
   - Join the lengthwise edges of two strips.
   - At the end of the seam, do not raise the presser foot or cut the threads. Butt the second set of strips to the first and continue sewing, chain stitching the strips together.
   - Continue, joining all the strip sets. Then clip the threads between the strips to separate the strips.
   - Subcut the strata into smaller blocks and join the blocks as directed.
   - Press the seams as indicated for each project.

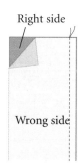
Right side

Wrong side

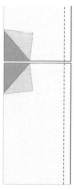
Butt strips; chain together

When the wind blows, the cradle will rock, and the Rock-a-Bye Baby Quilt will keep baby warm and comfortable. Using traditional seaming, this quilt is made with one basic block that is flip-flopped to create an interesting pattern that looks much more complicated than it really is. The quilt pictured uses cotton fabrics, but flannel would also be appropriate. What a great way to welcome a new baby into the world!

Note: The basic block used in this quilt is also used for the Fall into Fleece Throw (page 56) and the Vintage Romance Quilt (page 61). You'll love how versatile it is!

Rock-a-Bye Baby Quilt

Materials Needed Finished size: approximately 36" x 45"

- ¾ yd. Fabric A
- ½ yd. Fabric B
- 1¾ yd. Fabric C
- ½ yd. Fabric D

Making the Quilt

1. Cut the fabrics.
- Fabric A:
  - Cut five 2½" wide crosswise strips (pieced blocks).
  - Cut four 2½" wide crosswise strips (borders).
- Fabric B: Cut five 2½" wide crosswise strips (pieced blocks).
- Fabric C:
  - Cut three 2½" wide crosswise strips (pieced blocks).
  - Cut five 2½" wide crosswise strips (binding).
  - Save the remaining fabric for backing.
- Fabric D: Cut five 2½" wide crosswise strips (pieced blocks).

2. Set up the machine for traditional seaming.
- Attach a quilting foot such as the Patchwork Foot or Little Foot. As an option, adjust the needle position on the sewing machine to achieve a ¼" seam.

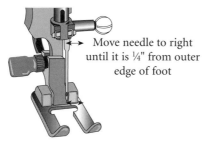

→ Move needle to right until it is ¼" from outer edge of foot

- Thread the needle and the bobbin with all-purpose sewing thread.
- Use a universal needle.
- Shorten the stitch length to 2.5 mm (12 stitches per inch).

3. Piece the blocks.
- Join the Fabric A and B strips.
  - Meet one Fabric A strip and one Fabric B strip, with right sides together, meeting the cut edges.
  - Stitch along one lengthwise edge.
  - Repeat for the remaining strips.
  - Subcut the A/B strips into 25 6½" long blocks. Press the seams flat, then to one side.
- Join the Fabric C strips to the A/B blocks.
  - Stack the A/B blocks, with right sides down, with the Fabric B section lying horizontally on top.
  - Place the Fabric C strips right sides up.
  - Place one A/B block on top of the Fabric C strip, with right sides together, placing the A/B block perpendicular to the lengthwise edge of the Fabric C strip.
  - Stitch a ¼" seam along the lengthwise edge. Guide the edge of the foot along the fabric edge to achieve uniform, precise seams.

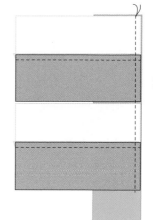

Fabric A right side

Fabric B wrong side

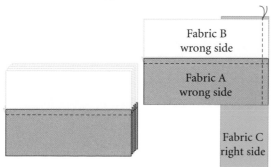

Fabric B wrong side

Fabric A wrong side

Fabric C right side

- At the end of the seam, place a second A/B block on the Fabric C strip, butting it to the first strip. Continue stitching.

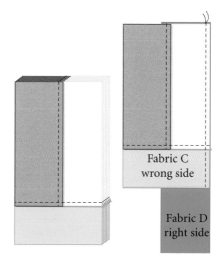

Butt second block; continue stitching

- Repeat, joining all the A/B blocks to the Fabric C strips.
- Cut the blocks apart, trimming away any extra Fabric C fabric between the blocks.
- Press the seams flat, then to one side.
- Join the Fabric D strips to the pieced blocks.
  - Stack the A/B/C blocks right sides down, with the Fabric C section lying horizontally on the bottom.
  - Place the Fabric D strips with right sides up.
  - Place one A/B/C block on top of the Fabric D strip, right sides together, placing the Fabric C section perpendicular to the lengthwise edge of the Fabric D strip.
  - Stitch the seam along the right edge.

Fabric C wrong side

Fabric D right side

- Butt a second block to the first block and continue stitching. Repeat, chain stitching all 25 blocks.
- Cut the blocks apart, trimming away any extra Fabric D fabric between the blocks.

- Press the seam allowances toward the Fabric D sections. Square up the edges of each block.

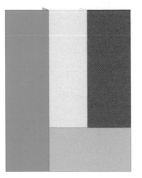

4. Assemble the quilt.
- Join the blocks into rows.
  - Arrange five rows, each containing five blocks, flip-flopping the blocks as shown to create the layout.

- Stitch the rows with right sides together.
- Press the seams in alternating directions in adjacent rows. This reduces bulk when the rows are joined.
- Join the rows, right sides together, aligning the seam intersections. Press the seams in one direction.

5. Add the borders.
- Square the quilt top, measuring from top to bottom, side to side, and corner to corner. Use a square quilting ruler to ensure that the corners are square.
- Meet and stitch Fabric A border strips to the left and right quilt edges, with right sides together. Trim the excess fabric even with the quilt edges. Press the seams toward the borders.

Add side borders

• Repeat, stitching the Fabric A border strips to the top and bottom quilt edges. Press the seams toward the borders.

6. Layer the quilt.

• Place the backing, wrong side up, on a firm surface such as a floor or some other flat surface. Securely tape the backing to the surface, using Sewer's Fix-it Tape or masking tape.

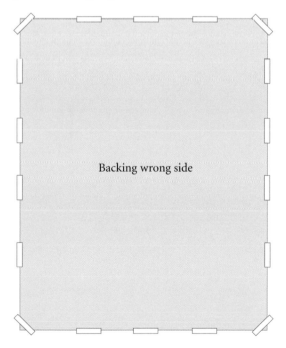

Backing wrong side

• Center the batting over the backing.
• Center the quilt, right side up, over the batting.

7. Pin the layers together using Size 1 Curved Basting Pins.

• Pin every 3" to 4".
• Place the pins no closer than ½" from the seams to allow room for the presser foot when machine quilting.
• Trim the excess batting and backing.

8. Quilt the quilt by machine or by hand.

• Machine quilt the quilt by stitching in the ditch through all the layers around each section, beginning in the center of the quilt and working toward the outer edges.

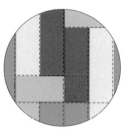

Stitch in the ditch

-OR-

• Hand tie the quilt using rayon ribbon floss, cotton embroidery floss, or yarn.

- Cut a long length of floss or yarn. Stitch at the corner of each block using a continuous thread.

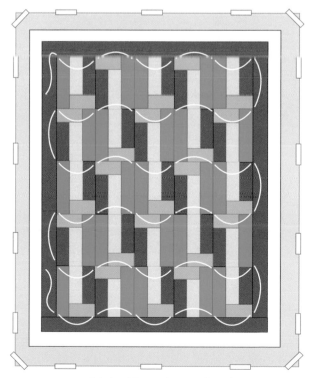

Stitch with continuous thread

- Cut a 2" to 3" thread tail at the first mark. Tie a square knot, first tying right over left; then left over right. Trim the thread tail to 2" to 3".
- Continue until all the knots are tied.
- Secure the knots with drops of Fray Check.

Clip threads, tie square knots

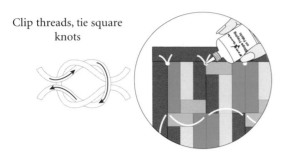

9. Bind the quilt.
- Join the Fabric C binding strips, with right sides together, seaming the strips on the diagonal to avoid bulk. Trim the seams to ¼".

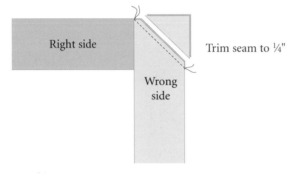

Right side

Trim seam to ¼"

Wrong side

- Cut one end of the strip at a 45° angle. Fold in ¼" at the trimmed end. Press a ¼" strip of paper-backed fusible web to the folded-under edge of the binding.

Fusible web

Wrong side

- Fold the binding in half lengthwise, with wrong sides together. Press.

Right side

- Mark the right side of the quilt ¼" from each corner.

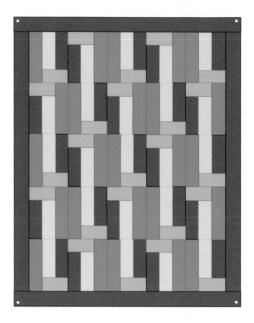

- Meet the angle-cut end of the binding (the end with the paper-backed fusible web) to the right side of the quilt, meeting the raw edges and starting in the center of one side. Stitch the binding to the quilt, beginning 4" from the end of the binding and stopping at the marked point at the first corner. Lock the stitches.

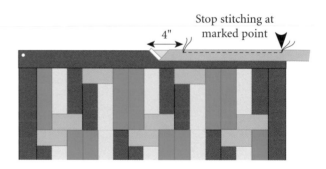

4"

Stop stitching at marked point

- Fold the binding up, aligning the cut edge of the binding with the cut edge of the quilt.

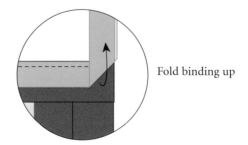

Fold binding up

- Fold the binding down, meeting the binding fold to the top edge of the quilt and the binding cut edge to the quilt side edges. Stitch the seam on the next side, starting at the folded edge.

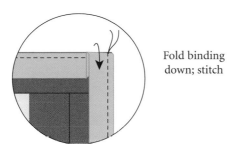

Fold binding down; stitch

- Repeat at the remaining corners.
- Join the binding ends.
  - Remove the paper backing from the binding.
  - Insert the free end of the binding inside the beginning of the binding so the binding is smooth and even with the quilt edge. Unfold the binding; trim the excess.
  - Press, fusing the binding ends together. Refold the binding.
  - Stitch the remainder of the binding seam.

Insert binding end; stitch

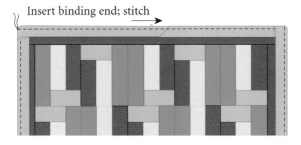

- Fold and press the binding away from the quilt. Then fold the binding to the wrong side, covering the stitching line and tucking in the corners to form miters. "Pin" the binding in place with Binding and Hem Clips.

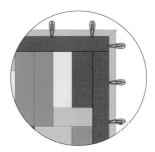

- Secure the remaining edge of the binding by stitching in the ditch from the right side, sewing in the well of the seam through all the layers to catch the folded edge on the back of the quilt. Or, hand stitch the folded edge to the wrong side of the quilt.

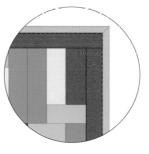

Give the gift of cozy warmth with the Fall into Fleece Throw. Make it in rich fall colors to please any man on your gift list. Whether he likes to curl up with a good book or the remote control, make sure that he'll be comfy and warm. Create the super-sized blocks for this throw using the same basic strip piecing techniques as for the Rock-a-Bye Baby Quilt, but this time cut wider strips and use simple serged flatlocked seaming. This throw is perfect for unwinding after a long day, sleeping away a lazy Sunday, or watching the big game. He's sure to enjoy it every season of the year!

Fall into Fleece Throw

Materials Needed
Finished size: approximately 66" x 78"

- ⅝ yd. Fabric A fleece
- ⅝ yd. Fabric B fleece
- ⅝ yd. Fabric C fleece
- 2 yd. Fabric D fleece

Making the Throw

1. Cut the fabrics.
   - Fabric A: Cut three 6" wide crosswise strips (pieced blocks).
   - Fabric B: Cut three 6" wide crosswise strips (pieced blocks).
   - Fabric C: Cut three 6" wide crosswise strips (pieced blocks).
   - Fabric D: Cut eleven 6" wide crosswise strips (pieced blocks and borders).

Note from Nancy

To easily cut through multiple layers of high-loft fleece, use a 60 mm rotary cutter held perpendicular to the ruler. Holding the cutter perpendicular compresses the fleece and minimizes stretching, making it easier to cut through the thick loft of the fleece.

Photo courtesy of Oxmoor House

2. Set up the machine for serged flatlocked seaming.
  - Set the machine for a two-thread flatlock stitch with the widest width and medium to long stitch length. ***Note:*** *Check your serger manual for specific instructions.*
  - Thread the machine with decorative thread both in the needle and lower looper.
  - Test the stitching with fabric scraps. Adjust the settings as needed.

Note from Nancy

You can also make this throw using other seaming options, such as kissed seaming or serged seaming. Kissed seaming is detailed for the Diamond Jubilee Scarf, page 67, using a standard sewing machine with an edge joining foot. Or, use a serger with a 3/4 thread overlock stitch.

3. Piece the blocks.
  - Join the Fabric A and B strips.
    - Meet one Fabric A and one Fabric B strip, with right sides together, aligning the cut edges. Flatlock along the lengthwise edge.

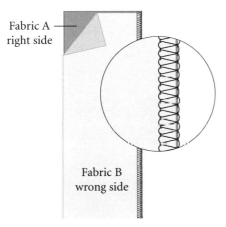

Fabric A right side

Fabric B wrong side

  - Repeat for the remaining strips.
    - Subcut the A/B strips into nine 18" long blocks.
    - Open the strip sets. Finger press to flatten the seams.
  - Join the Fabric C strips to the A/B blocks.
    - Stack the A/B blocks with right sides down, with the Fabric B section lying horizontally on top.
    - Place the Fabric C strips right sides up.
    - Place one A/B block on top of the Fabric C strip, with right sides together, placing the A/B block perpendicular to the lengthwise edge of the Fabric C strip. Serge the lengthwise edges.

  - Position the second A/B block on the Fabric C strip, allowing an approximate 1" space between the blocks. Because fleece sometimes stretches during stitching, this allows you to square up the blocks before joining them to another strip. Flatlock the edges. Continue until all the A/B blocks have been added to the Fabric C strips.

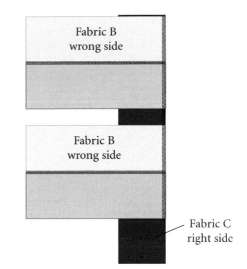

Fabric B wrong side

Fabric B wrong side

Fabric C right side

  - Cut the blocks apart, squaring the blocks with a quilting ruler and cutting away any extra Fabric C fabric.

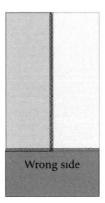

Wrong side

  - Open the strips. Finger press to flatten the seams.

- Join the Fabric D strips to the pieced blocks.
  - Stack the blocks, right sides down, with the Fabric C section lying horizontally on the bottom.
  - Place the Fabric D strips with right sides up.
  - Place one A/B/C block on the Fabric D strip, right sides together, placing the Fabric C section perpendicular to the lengthwise edge of the Fabric D strip. Flatlock the edges.
  - Place the second block on the Fabric D strip, allowing an approximate 1" space. Flatlock the edges. Continue until all the A/B/C blocks have been added to the Fabric D strips.
  - Cut the blocks apart, cutting away any extra Fabric D fabric.
  - Open the strips. Finger press to flatten the seams.
  - Square up the edges of each block.

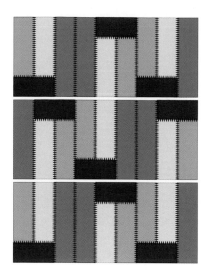

- Place a drop of seam sealant at each seam intersection.

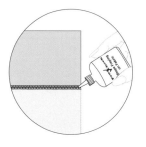

4. Assemble the throw.
   - Join the blocks into rows.
     - Arrange three rows of blocks, each containing three blocks, flip-flopping the blocks to create the layout.

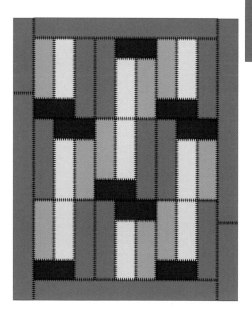

- Flatlock the rows with right sides together. Finger press to flatten the seams.
- Join the rows with right sides together. Finger press to flatten the seams.
- Add the borders.
  - Add the Fabric D borders to the top and bottom edges of the throw.
  - Cut one of the remaining Fabric D border strips in half.
  - Serge one half-strip to each remaining full strip.
  - Add the pieced borders to the left and right edges, positioning the half-strips at the opposite ends of the throw.

Stitch a quick pillowcase to coordinate with the Fall into Fleece Throw. The fabric is so soft and cuddly, it encourages sleeping in, especially on cold winter mornings. For a special touch, personalize the pillow with the recipient's initials. He'll be sure to thank you – if he can get out of bed!

Fall into Fleece Throw Pillow

Materials Needed   Finished size: approximately 24" x 30"

- ¼ yd. Fabric A fleece
- 1 yd. Fabric B fleece
- ¼ yd. Fabric C fleece
- ¼ yd. Fabric D fleece
- 18" x 24" pillow form

Making the Pillow

1. Cut the fabrics.
   - Fabric A: Cut one 6" x 18" rectangle (pieced block).
   - Fabric B:
     - Cut one 24" x 30" rectangle (pillow back).
     - Cut four 3" x 24" rectangles (borders).
     - Cut one 6" x 18" rectangle (pieced block).
   - Fabric C: Cut one 6" x 12" rectangle (pieced block).
   - Fabric D: Cut one 6" x 24" rectangle (pieced block).
2. Create the pillow top.
   - Piece one block as detailed for the Fall into Fleece Throw, page 56, using flatlocked seams.

- Add the borders.
  - Join two 3" x 24" Fabric B border rectangles to the top and bottom edges.

- Join the remaining 3" x 24" Fabric B border rectangles to the left and right edges.

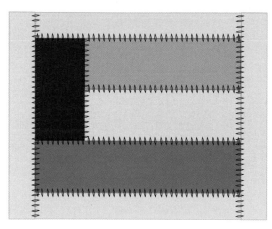

- Serge around the edges of the pillow top, with a 3/4 thread overlock stitch.

3. Embroider the pillow top.
   - To embroider a monogram, refer to your instruction manual to determine if your computerized machine has a built-in alphabet. If not, or if you don't like the look of the alphabet, use your favorite lettering program, such as Amazing Designs Lettering Pro. Or, purchase letter designs on disk, CD, or a memory card; or download designs from the Internet.
   - Embroider the monogram, using the hooping technique detailed for the Emerald Forest Throw Pillow, page 105.

4. Assemble the pillow.
   - Serge around the edges of the 24" x 30" Fabric B pillow back with a 3/4 thread overlock stitch.
   - Meet the pillow top and back with wrong sides together. Using a conventional sewing machine, stitch around three sides, sewing in the well of the seam around the pieced block. *Optional*: Use a zipper foot as a guide when sewing in the well of the seam.

Stitch three sides

- Insert the pillow form. Stitch the fourth side closed.

Stitch fourth side closed

The muted colors, ragged edges, and soft flannel of the Vintage Romance Quilt stir up sentimental memories of past romances, faded photos, and love letters tied with ribbon. The top and bottom of this quilt are stitched at the same time, making a reversible quilt with conventional seaming on one side and frayed-edge seaming on the other. The best part about this seaming technique is that your washer and dryer do part of the work! When you're finished stitching the quilt, just throw it in the laundry to enhance the frayed-edge effect. You'll love the soft look and feel of this technique – it's sure to capture the heart of the recipient!

Vintage Romance Quilt

Materials Needed   Finished size: approximately 53" x 69"

- 1 yd. Fabric A flannel
- 3¾ yd. Fabric B flannel
- 1⅛ yd. Fabric C flannel
- 4⅝ yd. Fabric D flannel

Making the Quilt

1. Cut the fabrics.
   - Fabric A: Cut six 5" wide crosswise strips (pieced blocks).
   - Fabric B:
     - Cut six 5" wide crosswise strips (pieced blocks).
     - Cut six 17" wide crosswise strips (heart block backgrounds). Subcut into 16 sections, 13" x 17".
   - Fabric C:
     - Cut four 5" wide crosswise strips (pieced blocks).
     - Cut twelve 3" wide crosswise strips (borders). Subcut four of the strips into four 3" x 14" and four 3" x 28" strips.
   - Fabric D:
     - Cut eight 5" wide crosswise strips (pieced blocks).
     - Cut seven 4" wide crosswise strips (binding).
     - Cut eight 11" wide crosswise strips (heart appliqués). Subcut into 16 blocks, 9" x 11".
     - Cut 16 hearts from the remaining fabric using the pattern on page 143.

2. Set up the sewing machine for frayed-edge seaming.
   - Adjust the machine for a ½" seam allowance. Although the traditional seam width for quilting is ¼", this frayed-edge technique uses ½" seams. Adjust the needle position so it is ½" from the right edge of the foot. If you cannot adjust the needle position, place tape on the bed of the machine ½" from the needle. Or, use a magnetic seam guide.
   - Set the machine for a short stitch length (15 to 18 stitches per inch).

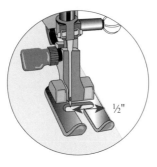

3. Create the pieced blocks.
   - Create combo strips of all four fabrics by stacking two strips of the same color, wrong sides together, to make reversible strips.

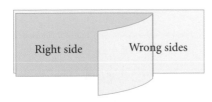

Right side   Wrong sides

- Join the Fabric A and B strips.
  - Join the Fabric A and B combo strips along the lengthwise edges, joining all four edges of the strips.

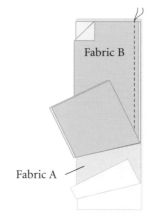

Fabric B

Fabric A

  - Subcut the A/B strips into eight 13" long blocks.
  - Press the seam allowances open by finger pressing or steam pressing.

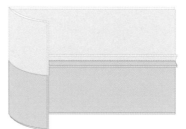

- Join the Fabric C Combo Strips to the Fabric A/B strips.
  - Stack the blocks, finished sides down, with the Fabric B section lying horizontally on top.
  - Align one A/B block to a Fabric C Combo Strip, placing the blocks perpendicular to the lengthwise edge of the Combo Strip, with the exposed seam side of the block on top. Stitch, making sure the pressed-open seams remain facing in the correct direction.

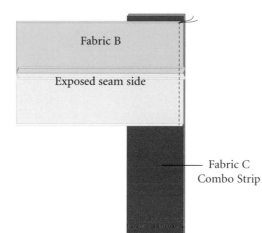

Fabric B

Exposed seam side

Fabric C
Combo Strip

- Press the seam allowances open by finger pressing or steam pressing.

Note from Nancy

To keep seams facing in the correct direction during seaming, use a stiletto or the point of a seam ripper to hold the seam allowances under the presser foot.

- Butt a second A/B block to the Fabric C Combo Strip and continue stitching.

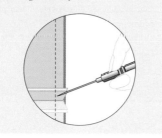

- Continue until all the A/B blocks are joined to the Fabric C Combo Strips.
- Cut the blocks apart, trimming away any extra Fabric C fabric between the blocks.

• Join the Fabric D Combo Strips to the pieced block.
  - Stack the blocks, finished sides down, with the Fabric C section lying horizontally on the bottom.
  - Align one A/B/C block to a Fabric D Combo Strip, placing the Fabric C section perpendicular to the lengthwise edge of the Combo Strip, with the exposed seam side of the block on top. Stitch, making sure the pressed-open seams remain facing in the correct direction.
  - Butt a second A/B/C block to the Fabric D Combo Strip and continue stitching.

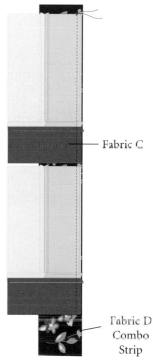

Fabric C

Fabric D
Combo
Strip

  - Continue until all the A/B/C blocks are joined to the Fabric D Combo Strips.
  - Cut the blocks apart, trimming away any extra Fabric D fabric between the blocks.
  - Press the seam allowances open by finger pressing or steam pressing. Square up the edges of each block.

4. Create eight heart blocks.

- Create eight Combo Blocks by stacking two 13" x 17" Fabric B blocks, wrong sides together.
- Stitch the heart blocks.
  - Center two 9" x 11" Fabric D rectangles, with wrong sides down, to one side of each Combo Block. Pin in place.
  - Center two cutout hearts on the opposite side of each Combo Block with wrong sides down. Adding two layers of fabric for the hearts adds body to the ragged edges of the hearts, matching the appearance of the rest of the quilt. The edges of the hearts must be more than ½" from the edges of the block. Securely pin the edges of the hearts.

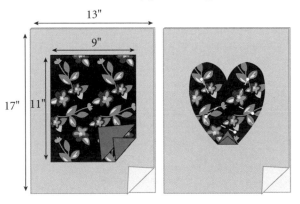

  - Position the needle ¼" from the outer edge of the presser foot. Stitch the heart to the Combo Block, guiding the edge of the presser foot along the fabric cut edge.
  - On the reverse side of the Combo Block, trim the excess Fabric D fabric ½" from the heart stitching line.

Trim ½" from stitching

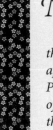

Note from Nancy

As an option, satin stitch along the edges of the cutout heart, treating it like a traditional appliqué. Trim the other side as directed. Place the satin stitched side on the underside of the quilt for a completely finished look on that side.

5. Arrange and join the quilt blocks.

- Arrange the blocks in four rows.
  - Row 1: Heart Block, Pieced Block, Heart Block, Pieced Block
  - Row 2: Pieced Block, Heart Block, Pieced Block, Heart Block
  - Row 3: Heart Block, Pieced Block, Heart Block, Pieced Block
  - Row 4: Pieced Block, Heart Block, Pieced Block, Heart Block

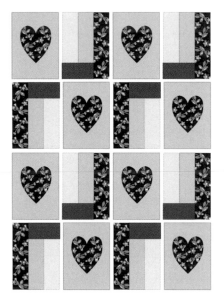

- Join the four blocks in each row, making certain all the seam allowances face the same side. Press the seams open.

- Join the four rows. There will be a lot of fabric at the seam intersections. Backstitch at those points to reinforce the stitching for added durability. Press the seams open.

6. Attach the borders.
- Join a 3" x 14" Fabric C strip and a 3" wide Fabric C crosswise strip with a ¼" seam. Repeat with the three remaining 3" x 14" strips for a total of four 3" x approximately 56" strips.
- Join a 3" x 28" Fabric C strip and a 3" wide Fabric C crosswise strip with a ¼" seam. Repeat with the three remaining 3" x 28" strips for a total of four 3" x approximately 70" strips.

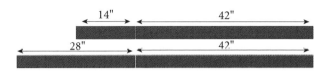

- Create a 3" x 56" Combo Strip by stacking two strips with wrong sides together. Repeat with the remaining 3" x 56" strips.
- Create a 3" x 70" Combo Strip by stacking two strips, with wrong sides together. Repeat with the remaining 3" x 70" strips.
- Join the 3" x 70" Fabric C Combo Strips to the left and right edges of the quilt. Remember, all frayed-edge seam allowances must be on one side of the quilt. Press the seam allowances open. Trim the excess.
- Join the 3" x 56" Fabric C Combo Strips to the top and bottom edges of the quilt. Press the seam allowances open. Trim the excess.

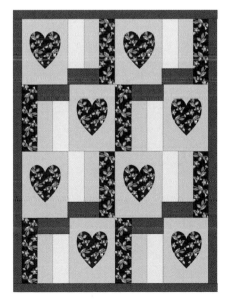

7. Bind the quilt.
- Prepare the binding strips.
  - Join the Fabric D binding strips, right sides together, with diagonal seams to reduce bulk. Trim the seams to ¼".

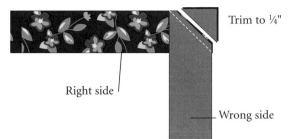

  - Cut one end of the strip at a 45° angle. Fold in ¼" at the trimmed end.
  - Fold the binding in half, wrong sides together, meeting the lengthwise edges. Press.

- Mark the quilt top ½" from each corner on the underside of the quilt.

Mark ½" from corners

- Pin the binding to the underside of the quilt, meeting the fold of the binding to the cut edge of the quilt, starting in the center of one side.
- Stitch the binding to the quilt, stopping the stitching at the marked point at the first corner. Lock the stitches.

Stop stitching at marked point

- Fold the binding up at a 45° angle, aligning the folded edge of the binding with the cut edge of the quilt.
- Fold the binding down, meeting the fold of the binding to the top edge of the quilt and the binding outer folded edge to the quilt side edges. Stitch a ½" seam on the second side, starting at the folded edge.

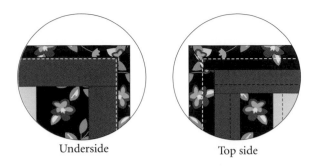

Underside   Top side

Fold binding up   Fold binding down; stitch

- Repeat at the remaining corners. Overlap the binding at the starting point and trim the excess.
- Fold and press the binding to the top side of the quilt, covering the unfinished edges and extending approximately ½" beyond the seamline. Pin. **Note:** *The raw edge of the binding will be visible on the right side.*
- Secure the binding by stitching in the ditch from the underside of the quilt, sewing in the well of the seam through all the layers to catch the free edge of the binding.

8. Fray the seams.
- Clip all the exposed seam allowances and binding edges every ¼" to ½", stopping prior to the stitching line. If you accidentally clip the stitching line, go back and restitch that section. When clipping the seam areas, be sure to clip each seam edge.

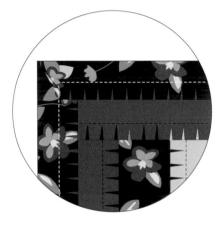

- Wash the quilt, or put it through the rinse cycle. Then place it in the dryer for 15 minutes.

Note from Nancy

It's important to empty the lint filter after each 15 minute drying cycle. You'll be amazed at how much lint accumulates!

- Repeat 15 minute drying cycles until the quilt is completely dry, making certain to empty the lint filter prior to each cycle.
- For additional fraying, repeat the washing and drying process.

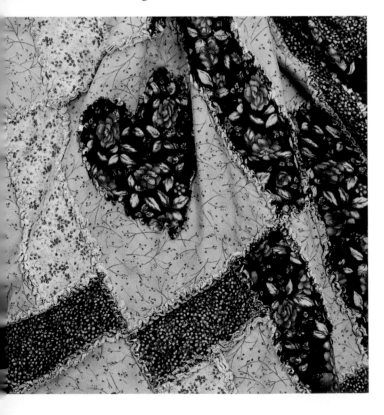

Diamond Jubilee Scarf

Who wouldn't love diamonds as a gift? When you make this scarf, you can give your friends diamonds without spending several months' salary! On this scarf, the traditional diamond shaping is created in a new and novel way, with kissed edge-joined seams. No matter what the occasion — even if it's just a cold day and you have leftover fleece — giving this scarf as a gift will always call for a joyous celebration!

Materials Needed   Finished size: approximately 13½" x 69"

- ½ yd. Fabric A fleece
- ⅓ yd. Fabric B fleece

Making the Scarf

1. Cut the fabrics.
   - Fabric A:
     - Cut two 7" x 14" rectangles (fringe).
     - Cut two 1" wide crosswise strips (borders).
     - Cut three 3½" wide crosswise strips (strata).

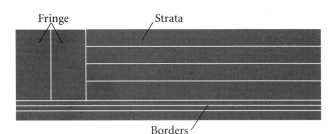

Fringe   Strata

Borders

   - Fabric B: Cut three 3½" wide crosswise strips (strata).

Note from Nancy

To easily cut through multiple layers of high-loft fleece, use a 60 mm rotary cutter held perpendicular to the ruler. (See photo on page 56.)

2. Make the fringe on the two 7" x 14" Fabric A rectangles.
   - Wrap 1" of the 14" edge around the edge of a rotary cutting mat.

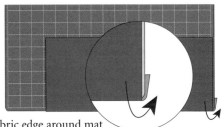

Wrap fabric edge around mat

   - Use a rotary cutter to cut fringes ½" apart on the remainder of the 14" edge.

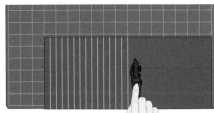

Cut fringe at ½" increments

3. Prepare a strata by joining the 3½" strips with kissed edge-joined seams.
   - Arrange the strips in the following order: A, B, A, B, A, B. Check that all the strips are right side up. (Remember, fleece curls to the wrong side when it is stretched on the crossgrain.)

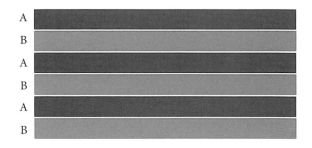

   - Set up the sewing machine for kissed edge-joined seaming.
     - Thread both the top and bobbin with all-purpose thread.
     - Replace the presser foot with the edge joining foot. A guide in the center of this foot keeps fabrics precisely aligned for even stitching.
     - Use a balanced tension.

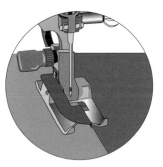

     - Set the machine for a feather stitch or a multi-zigzag with a length of 2.0 and a width of 6.0. Or, use a wide zigzag and shorten the length to 1.0.
     - Test the stitching with fabric scraps. Adjust the settings as necessary.
   - Stitch the strips together.
     - Butt the cut edges of the adjoining fleece strips together; slide the guide on the edge joining foot between the two butted edges to ensure that the stitching is centered as the two pieces are seamed.
     - Seam the strips together in the sequence listed above, taking care to avoid stretching the fabrics.
     - Seal the thread tail ends with a tiny drop of seam sealant such as Fray Check. Then cut the threads even with the fleece edges.

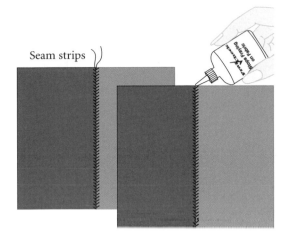

Seam strips

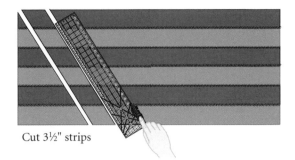

- Steam press the strata, being careful not to touch the iron to the fabric to avoid damaging the surface of the fabric.

Note from Nancy

You can also make this scarf using different seaming options, such as serged flat-locked seams, which are detailed for the Fall into Fleece Throw, page 56.

4. Cross-cut diamond shapes from the seamed strips.
   - Place the strata horizontally on a cutting mat.
   - Align the 60° marking on a quilting ruler along one lengthwise edge of the strata, positioning the ruler so its edge meets the left corner of the strata. Cut along that line. Getting those two positions precisely aligned is important! If the angle isn't correct, it will be difficult to get the diamonds to match.

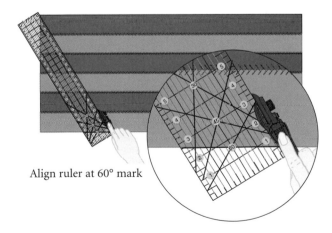

Align ruler at 60° mark

   - Move the ruler over 3½", keeping the 60° mark aligned along the edge of the strata. Cut again.

- Repeat, cutting eight strips. (If you want to make the scarf longer, you need to cut additional strips. You always need an even number of strips.)

Cut 3½" strips

5. Join the strips to shape the scarf.
   - Join the short ends of each strip with an edge-joined seam, stitching each strip into a tube.

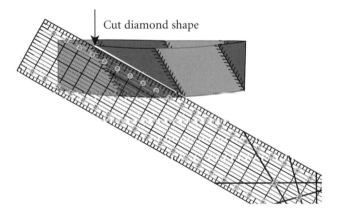

Join strip ends

   - Cut one Fabric A diamond shape down the center, from tip to tip, using a ruler. This shapes the end. Repeat on the remaining strips, always cutting a Fabric A diamond.

Cut diamond shape

   - Align all eight strips, butting the long cut edges together.
   - Stitch the strips together, using kissed edge-joined seams.

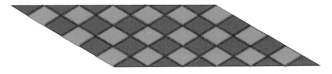

• Cut one diamond shape down the center, cutting through Fabric A.

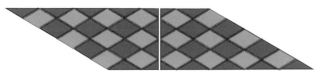

• Join the angled ends of the strips to form a straight panel with square ends.

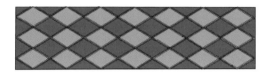

6. Add borders to the scarf.
  • Tape-baste the 1" wide Fabric A borders to the scarf using Sewer's Fix-it Tape. Stitch, using kissed edge-joined seams. Tape-basting will increase accuracy and keep the sections in place. Remove the tape as you come to it; do not stitch through the tape.

• Trim the excess borders even with the scarf ends.

Cut off excess border length

7. Seam the fringe panels to the ends of the scarf using edge-joined seams. *Optional:* Pull the fringe to make it curl.

Optional: Pull fringe to curl

Playing outside in the winter, especially after a snowfall, is great fun, but mittens often don't cover enough of the forearm to prevent snow from accumulating between the mitten and the arm. These extended, too-tall mittens are just what you need. Add a diamond appliqué and an accent band to coordinate with the Diamond Jubilee Scarf and you'll have a great winter set all ready to wrap up and put under the tree!

Diamond Jubilee Mittens

Materials Needed

- ½ yd. Fabric A fleece
- Scraps of Fabric B fleece (diamond appliqués)
- ½ yd. stretch binding (or more depending on wrist measurement)
- Pressure-sensitive paper-backed fusible web (AppliqEase Lite)

Making the Mittens

1. Prepare the pattern.
- Fold a piece of Pattern Paper, longer than the desired mitten size, in half.
- Trace an existing mitten shape on the paper (or trace the hand shape on the paper), aligning the outer straight edge of the hand along the fold. Mark the wrist position.

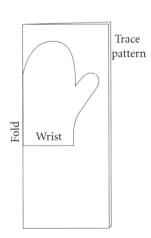

Trace pattern

Fold

Wrist

Note from Nancy

Don't make the mitten too tight. You want to be sure to have a little ease for wearing comfort. If you trace your hand, make sure the opening of the mitten is at least as wide as the widest part of your hand. Otherwise, you will not be able to slip your hand into the mitten.

- Extend the length of the mitten 4" to 6" from the wrist mark.
- Add a ¼" seam allowance around the drawn shape.
- Cut out and unfold the pattern.

2. Cut out the mittens.
- Fold the fleece in half, with the stretch of the fabric in the crosswise direction.
- Place the pattern on the fleece and cut out two mittens. Mark the wrist position.

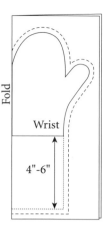

Extend length; add seam allowances

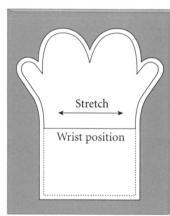

3. Add double needle stitching to the cuff of each mitten. A double needle requires a zigzag sewing machine and has two needles attached to a single needle shaft. On the right side of the fabric, a single row of stitching produces two perfectly parallel rows of stitching. On the wrong side, a single bobbin thread moves back and forth between the two needle threads, resembling a zigzag.
- Set up the machine for double needle stitching.
  - Insert a size 3.0 mm/90 or 4.0 mm/90 double needle. The first number in a double needle designation refers to the distance in millimeters between the two needles, while the second number refers to the size of the needle.
  - Slightly loosen the top thread tensions by one number or notch. This prevents the bobbin thread from being drawn to the right side of the fabric.
  - Thread the machine with thread matched to the fleece. Thread the two top threads through the machine as if they were a single thread and separate them at the needles, inserting one through each needle.
- Stitch one row of horizontal double needle stitching across the top of the mitten cuff to establish the cuff line.

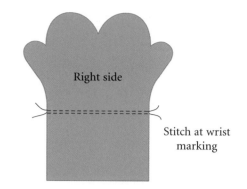

Stitch at wrist marking

- Use double needle stitching to simulate ribbing.
  - Begin at the lower edge ½" from the side edge and stitch to the horizontal cuff line.

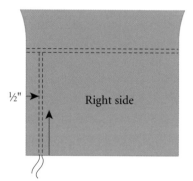

- Raise the presser foot and the needle; gently turn the fabric. Pivot and stitch four to five stitches along the horizontal row.

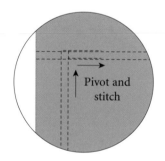

- Pivot again and stitch back down the cuff, sewing parallel to the previous row of stitching.

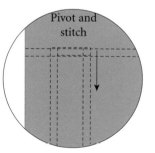

- Repeat until the entire cuff has been double-needle stitched.

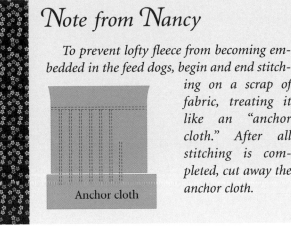
4. Prepare the diamond appliqués.
- Trace two diamonds onto the paper side of AppliqEase Lite, using the pattern on page 143.

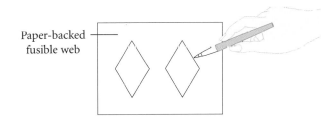

Paper-backed fusible web

AppliqEase has a repositionable fusible webbing. A pressure sensitive coating on one side of the web allows this fusible to "stick," enabling you to easily position the diamond appliqués before permanently stitching them in place.
- Roughly cut out the diamonds, allowing approximately ¼" margins around all the outer edges. Fuse the diamonds to the wrong side of the Fabric B fleece.

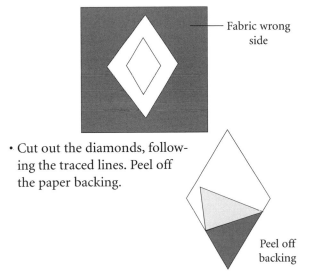

Fabric wrong side

- Cut out the diamonds, following the traced lines. Peel off the paper backing.

Peel off backing

- Place the diamonds on the right side of the fabric, positioning the bottom point approximately ¼" above the horizontal stitching line. On one mitten, place the diamond on the right portion. On the other mitten, place the diamond on the left portion. This way, you have both left and right mittens.

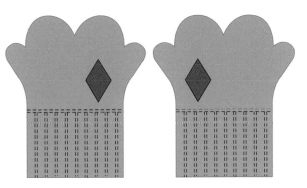

5. Appliqué the diamonds to the mitten.
- Set up the sewing machine for blanket stitch appliqué.
  - Attach an open toe foot.
  - Thread the top of the machine with rayon or cotton machine embroidery thread. Use a lightweight thread such as Madeira Bobbinfil or prewound bobbins in the bobbin.

  - Adjust the machine for a blanket stitch with a wide stitch width and a short stitch length. Test the stitching on a sample; the straight portion of the stitch should follow the edge of the appliqué and the "zig" portions of the stitch should extend into the appliqué. Adjust the stitch width and length as necessary to achieve the desired look.

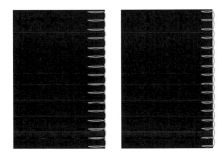

- Align the appliqué with the inner edge of the presser foot toe. Stitch around the diamond.
  - When about ½" from the point of the diamond, gradually narrow the stitch width to avoid having the "zig" of the stitch extend beyond the appliqué edges.
  - At the point of the diamond, stop with the needle down in the fabric.

- Pivot and continue stitching, gradually returning the stitch width to the normal setting.

- Repeat until the entire diamond is appliquéd.

6. Add stretch binding to the lower edge.
  - Cut a length of stretch binding ½" longer than the lower edge. This binding is a soft, two-way stretch 1⅝" wide binding that shapes easily along edges. It's a great way to add a fashion accent and finishing touch in one easy step.
  - Pin the binding along the lower edge of the mitten at a 1:1 ratio with right sides together.

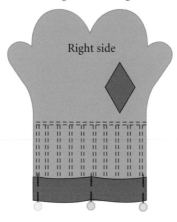

Right side

- Stitch the binding to the mitten, guiding the presser foot along the cut edges.

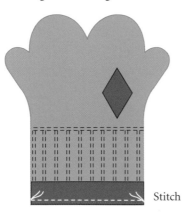

Stitch

- Wrap the binding to the wrong side so it is a consistent width. Pin the binding in place from the right side.

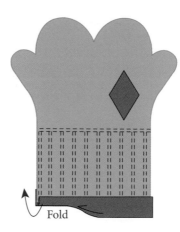

Fold

- Stitch in the ditch from the right side, sewing in the well of the seam to secure the binding. If necessary, trim away the excess binding on the wrong side.

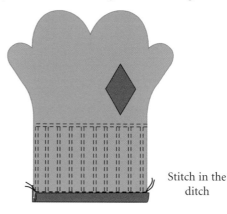

Stitch in the ditch

7. Fold the mitten in half, right sides together, aligning the horizontal stitching. Stitch the side seam using a ¼" seam. Restitch the thumb area for reinforcement.

8. Clip to the inner corner at the thumb.

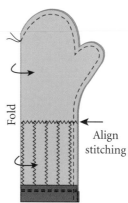

Fold

Align stitching

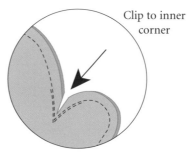

Clip to inner corner

9. Turn the mitten right side out.

Add some points of interest to a set of towels with the Golden Glow Towels. These towels feature a richly colored chevron accent band which was created with Seminole Patchwork, a quilting method named after Florida's Seminole Indians who originated the technique. You can make the band with as many strips as you prefer in colors to coordinate with a friend's décor. If finding the perfect gift has you ready to throw in the towel, look no further than the Golden Glow Towels. They make a wonderful gift – or the perfect accent for your bathroom!

Golden Glow Towels

Materials Needed

- ¼ yd. Fabric A
- ¼ yd. Fabric B
- ¼ yd. Fabric C

- Tear-away stabilizer
- *Optional:* Temporary spray adhesive

Making the Seminole Appliqué

1. Cut the strips.
   - Fabric A: Cut four 2" wide crosswise strips.
   - Fabric B: Cut eight ¾" wide crosswise strips.
   - Fabric C: Cut six 1½" wide crosswise strips.

Note from Nancy

Part of the fun of working with Seminole patchwork is that you have so much flexibility. Change the fabrics, the width of the strips, and how you cut the strips – you'll be amazed at the different looks you get. One bit of advice: don't make any strip narrower than ¾" or it won't be visible in the finished strata.

2. Create two stratas for the chevron design.
- Divide the strips, right sides up, into two equal stacks. Using a quilting ruler, cut one end of one strip stack at a 45° angle.

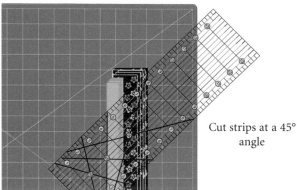

Cut strips at a 45° angle

- Flip over the ruler and cut a mirror image 45° angle at one end of the second strip stack.

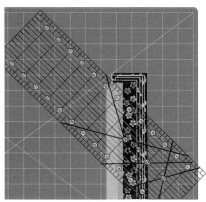

Flip ruler and cut mirror image

- Arrange the strips, creating a strata from each stack with the following configuration: ABCBCBCBA.

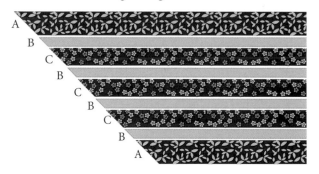

- Join the strips, right sides together, with ¼" seams. Start each seam at the angle-cut end, offsetting the ends of the two strips ¼". A small triangle extends on one fabric. The finished stratas will have an angled appearance at one end.

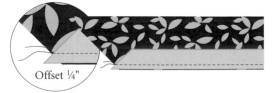

Offset ¼"

- Press the seam allowances of one strata in one direction. Press the seam allowances on the second strata in the opposite direction. Trim the small seam allowance triangles that extend at the ends of the strips.

3. Cross-cut the chevron strips.
- Meet the stratas, right sides together, matching the cut edges and seamlines.
- Using a quilting ruler, cut an accurate 45° angle at one end of the strata. Because the ends of the strips were angle-cut and the seams offset, there is little waste.

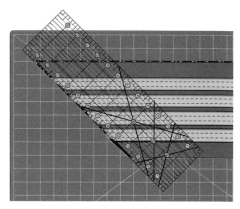

- Cut 2½" wide strips, measuring from the 45° angle-cut edge. Keep the cut pairs together.

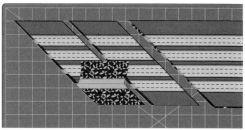

Cut 2½" strips

4. Stitch the pairs together.
- Pin the pairs together; check that seams are aligned and the seam allowances are facing in opposite directions.
- Stitch along one edge with a ¼" seam.
  - Adjust the stitch length to 12 to 15 stitches per inch.
  - Use a stiletto or seam ripper to keep the seam allowances facing in the right direction and to keep the edges straight.
- Chain stitch the pairs together, checking that the chevrons meet.
- Clip the thread tails between the pairs. Press the seams flat, then in one direction.

Join pairs

Wrong side

• Stitch the pairs together, creating a long Seminole patch. Press the seams flat; then in one direction.

Join
pairs

5. Position the appliqué strip on the towel. Use an adhesive spray such as Dritz Spray Adhesive to hold the strip in place, lightly spraying the wrong side of the strip. Or, pin and straight stitch the strip to the towel to secure it for satin stitching.

Spray
wrong side

6. Satin stitch the Seminole design to the towel.
• Thread the top of the machine with cotton embroidery thread.
• Adjust the machine for a satin stitch using a medium width and a short stitch length.
• Place a tear-away stabilizer on the wrong side of the towel, under the edges of the appliqué band. Satin stitch the band in place.

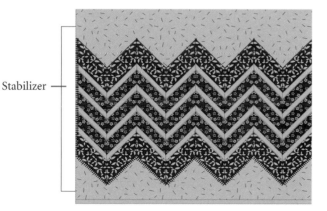

Stabilizer

7. *Optional*: If the design is very long, you may want to stitch along the middle of the design with monofilament thread to stabilize the strip to the towel.

8. For the smaller towel, make the following modifications:
• Cut the fabrics.
  - Fabric A: Cut four 1½" wide crosswise strips.
  - Fabric B: Cut eight ¾" wide crosswise strips.
  - Fabric C: Cut four 1½" wide crosswise strips.
• Arrange the strips with the following configuration: ABCBCBA.

9. For a washcloth, cross-cut one strip and satin stitch it in place.

If diamonds are a girl's best friend, then wouldn't she love a set of cosmetic bags featuring rows of richly colored diamonds? To create the diamond accent bands, simply stitch a modified version of the Seminole quilted band used for the towels. The larger bag is made with quilted fabric, while the smaller one features novelty fabrics so you can see at a glance what's inside. Although these bags don't have as many carats as real jewels, with them as your travel companions you can transport your cosmetics in style.

Black Diamonds Cosmetic Bag

Materials Needed Approximate finished size: 9" x 12"

- ⅛ yd. Fabric A
- ½ yd. Fabric B
- ⅛ yd. Fabric C
- ⅓ yd. batting
- 9" zipper or longer
- *Optional:* ⅛" x 4" strip of synthetic suede for zipper pull

Making the Bag

1. Create the diamond Seminole accent band.
- Cut the fabrics.
  - Fabric A: Cut one 2" wide crosswise strip.
  - Fabric B: Cut one 1½" wide crosswise strip.
  - Fabric C: Cut one 2" wide crosswise strip.
- Arrange the strips to create a strata with the following configuration: ABC.

- Join the strips, right sides together, with ¼" seams. Press the seam allowances in one direction.

- Cut the strata into 1½" wide sections.
- Take two sections. Offset the two sections by moving one piece down the width of the Fabric B strip. Meet the sections, right sides together, making sure the circled intersection is matched. Stitch, using a ¼" seam allowance.

1½"

Match intersection

- Chain stitch the sections together until you have one long piece.
- Clip the sections apart. Make two stacks of section pairs, keeping the colors in order.
- Take one pair from each stack; offset the two pairs by moving one pair down the width of one Fabric B strip. Meet the pairs, right sides together, making sure the circled intersection is matched.

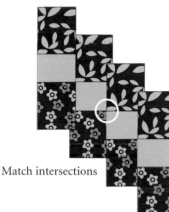

Match intersections

- Chain stitch the pairs together. Clip the pairs apart.
- Repeat until all the pairs are joined. Press all the seam allowances in the same direction.
- Straighten the edge of the Seminole strip. In order to use the entire Seminole strip, the ends of the piece should be straightened. Check the piece to see if there is one intersection where the seamlines don't match. If there is, make a cut there along the straight of the grain. Place a ruler on the piece and cut.

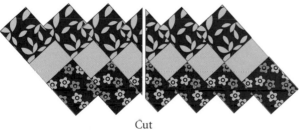

Cut

- Stitch the two bias cut ends together, right sides together, matching the seam intersections and offsetting the sections as before. Stitch.

2. Cut the fabrics for the bag.
   - Upper front section: Trim the Seminole strip to 2½" x 8", centering the Fabric B diamonds in the center of the strip. Cut a 2½" x 8" rectangle from Fabric B for the backing.

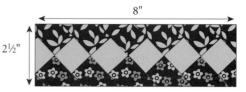

   - Lower front section: Cut two 8" squares from Fabric B.
   - Back section: Cut two 8" x 12" rectangles from Fabric B.

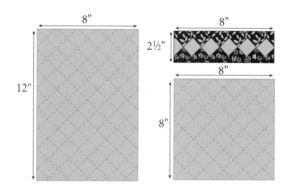

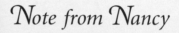

Note from Nancy

To quilt the three bag sections, cut a layer of batting the same size as each section. Layer the batting between the two fabric layers for each section, then stitch a grid to quilt the layers together.

3. Insert a zipper.
   - Open the zipper. Meet one of the 8" sides of the lower front section to one of the zipper tape edges, with right sides together. Attach a zipper foot; stitch a ¼" to ½" seam to attach one side of the zipper.

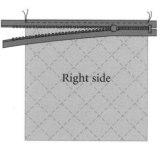

Right side

- Close the zipper. Align the outer edges of the upper and lower front sections. Position and stitch the remaining zipper tape edge to an 8" edge of the upper front section with right sides together.
- Partially open the zipper.

Wrong side

4. Meet the back section to the front section, right sides together, meeting the top and bottom edges. Stitch or serge along the top and bottom edges. **Note:** *The back section is longer than the front section, so there will be excess fabric in the back.*

Wrong side

Stitch top and bottom

5. Meet the side edges. Stitch or serge along the side edges. Cut off the excess zipper length.

Stitch sides; cut off excess zipper

6. Form a gusset at the lower edge.
- At each corner, fold the fabric so the side seam stacks on top of the lower fold, forming a triangle.

- Stitch perpendicular to the seam 1" from the point, reinforcing the stitching at each end.

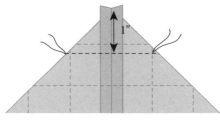

1"

7. Turn the bag right side out through the zipper opening.

8. *Optional*: Create a zipper pull.
- Fold the ⅛" x 4" synthetic suede strip in half.
- Thread the fold through the hole on the zipper pull tab.
- Insert the ends through the loop and pull on the ends to tighten the loop.

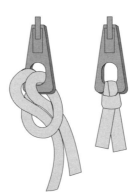

Make the smaller version of the Black Diamonds Cosmetic Bag to complete your stylish set. Instead of quilted fabric, use clear vinyl and charcoal fiberglass screen to create the bag. The construction is the same – only the fabrics and the dimensions change.

Perfect for a trip to the gym or a tropical island escape, these bags make excellent gifts for friends, or for you!

Small Bag

Materials Needed	Finished size folded: approximately 6" x 9"

- ⅛ yd. Fabric A
- ⅛ yd. Fabric B
- ⅛ yd. Fabric C
- ¼ yd. clear vinyl

- ¼ yd. charcoal fiberglass screen
- 7" zipper or longer
- Seminole accent band

Making the Bag

1. Create the diamond Seminole accent band as detailed on pages 78-79.
2. Cut out the fabric pieces for the bag.
   - Upper front section: Trim the Seminole strip to 2½" x 6½", centering the Fabric B diamonds in the center of the strip.
   - Lower front section: Cut a 6½" square from both clear vinyl and charcoal fiberglass screen.
   - Back section: Cut a 6½" x 10½" rectangle from both clear vinyl and charcoal fiberglass screen.
3. Construct the bag the same as the larger bag with the following modifications.
   - Layer the clear vinyl and fiberglass screen to create the lower front and back sections. Treat the two layers as one piece of fabric, with the fiberglass screen as the right side, and the clear vinyl as the wrong side. ***Note:*** *Do not quilt the bag sections.*
   - Create a gusset at the lower edge as detailed for the larger bag, stitching ½" from the point.

Note from Nancy

Fiberglass screen and vinyl may seem like unusual fabric choices, but they're both as easy to sew as any other fabric. Charcoal fiberglass screen is the same material you find in your window screens! But we've found that it works just as well in a variety of sewing projects. It won't dull your needle or leave a residue on your needle. It sews just like regular fabric! Clear vinyl is also a fun material, and pairing it with the screen adds a unique element to your cosmetic bags. I'm sure you'll enjoy making gifts with these fun "fabrics."

Store your jewelry in classic elegance with this unique tray that is equal parts function and form. Lined with clear vinyl for stability, it will add an artistic element to your dresser top or bathroom counter. Paired with the Golden Glow Towels and Black Diamond Cosmetic Bags, you can quickly create a coordinating set – a perfect housewarming or bridal shower gift!

Shades of Sophistication Jewelry Tray

Materials Needed   Finished size folded: approximately 4" x 6" x 2½"

- ⅛ yd. Fabric A
- ⅜ yd. Fabric B
- ⅛ yd. Fabric C

- ⅜ yd. clear vinyl
- Four frog closures
- Seminole accent band

Making the Basket

1. Create the diamond Seminole accent band as detailed for the Black Diamonds Cosmetic Bag, pages 78-79.
2. Cut the fabrics.
   - Fabric B:
     - Cut two 10" x 12" rectangles (tray interior and exterior).
     - Cut 2½" wide bias strips to total approximately 1½ yards binding.
   - Clear vinyl: Cut one 10" x 12" rectangle (tray lining).
   - Batting: Cut one 10" x 12" rectangle.

3. Prepare the pattern.
   - Cut a 9" x 11" rectangle from Pattern Paper.
   - Trim away a 2½" square from each corner.

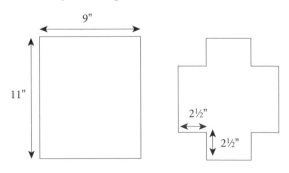

4. Layer and quilt the tray.
  • Layer the Fabric B rectangles and batting. Pin together.

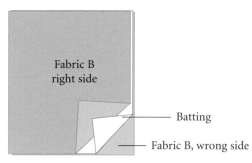

Fabric B
right side

Batting

Fabric B, wrong side

  • Center the pattern on the fabric sandwich. Mark the inner corners.

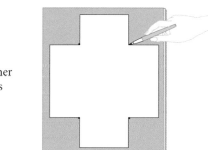

Mark inner
corners

  • Remove the pattern and draw lines both horizontally and vertically to connect the marks with a fabric marking pencil.

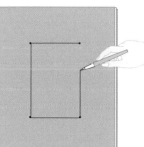

Draw lines

  • Stitch along the marked lines, creating "memory lines." These lines provide a guide for quilting.
  • Quilt a grid, following the memory lines, spacing the lines approximately 1½" apart.

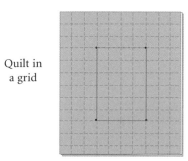

Quilt in
a grid

  • Position the pattern on the quilted fabric sandwich, aligning the edges so they are parallel to the quilting lines. Cut out the pattern.

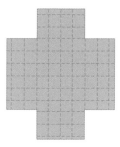

5. Add the Seminole patchwork accent strips.
  • Position a ruler on the wrong side of the Seminole strip, positioning it along the points of the Fabric B diamonds.

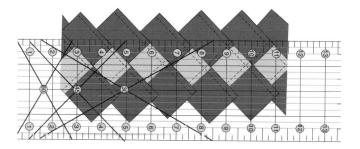

  • Fold the loose points over the edge of the ruler. Press.

Fold

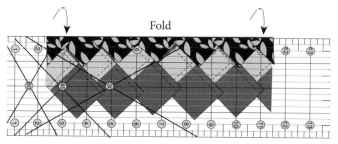

Note from Nancy

A handy tool to use for pressing the Seminole strip is the Ezy-Hem Gauge. Simply position the straight edge of the gauge along the diamond points and keep it there while you press. Heat from an iron will not damage the gauge, so you can measure and press in one easy step! After pressing, take care when removing the gauge from your fabric. Use a cloth to pick it up, or let it cool off, so you don't burn yourself.

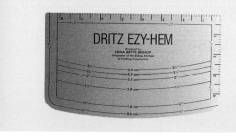

DRITZ EZY-HEM

- Measuring from the fold, cut the strip to 2¼" wide.
- Subcut the strip into two 4¼" lengths and two 6¼" lengths.

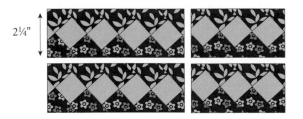

- Position the rectangles on the tray flaps, aligning the cut edges. Edgestitch close to the folds.

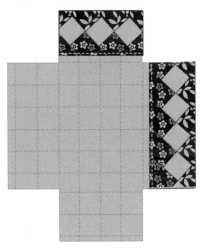

6. Add the clear vinyl lining.
- Cut one pattern from clear vinyl, keeping the paper attached.

Note from Nancy

Leaving the paper backing on the clear vinyl makes it easier to feed the vinyl through the sewing machine.

- Position the clear vinyl on the back of the quilted tray, meeting the vinyl side to the fabric.
- Stitch together along the original "memory" lines.
- Staystitch all the layers together, stitching ¼" from the edges.
- Clip into the interior corners without cutting through the staystitching.

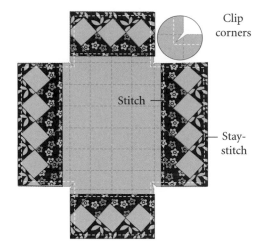

Clip corners

Stitch

Stay-stitch

7. Prepare the binding strips as detailed for the Rock-a-Bye Baby Quilt, page 54.

8. Bind the tray.
- Mark the interior of the tray ¼" from each inside and outside corner. Position the binding on the interior of tray, beginning on an outer edge.

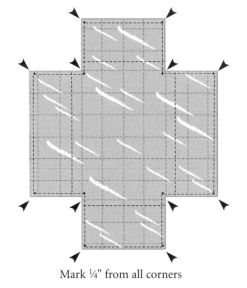

Mark ¼" from all corners

- Bind the quilt as detailed for the Rock-a-Bye Baby Quilt, pages 54-55. Follow those instructions for turning the outside corners.
- When you come to an inside corner:
  - Stop stitching at the marked point, leaving the needle down in the fabric.

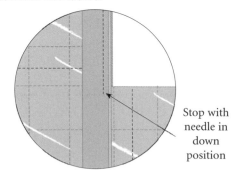

Stop with needle in down position

- Gently pivot the fabric under the binding so the second side of the cutout aligns with the edge of the binding. Continue stitching to the next corner mark.

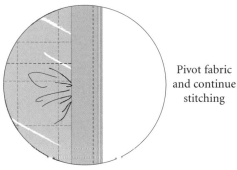

Pivot fabric and continue stitching

Note from Nancy

It's sometimes difficult to tell whether the stitching has caught the fabric at the pivot point on the underside. After you're past the corner, stop with the needle down in your fabric and check to ensure you caught the fabric at the pivot point. If not, you can easily go back and restitch.

• Repeat the steps at the remaining corners. Fold the binding to the exterior of the tray, aligning the pressed edge so it covers the stitching line and tucking the corners to form miters. Edgestitch the tape in place.

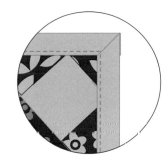

9. Position the closures (frog closures or elastic hair bands) on each side of the tray, approximately halfway down the side. Hand stitch the closures in place.

CHAPTER 4

Enchanting Embroidery

Nancy drew a little sketch,
A snowy winter scene;
Embroidered it by hand and then
She stitched it by machine.

When you look at a spool of thread or skein of embroidery floss, it's sometimes hard to imagine the creative possibilities that are woven into their very fibers. But give these tools to an embroiderer, notice the twinkle in her eye, and just wait to see the breathtaking projects she creates.

In this chapter, make exquisite gifts showcasing thread and embroidery floss. From elegant table linens to stunning frames, these projects are sure to enchant and amaze their recipients. You won't believe how simple these projects really are. And just think; they all start with a spool or skein of thread and a twinkle of inspiration.

Embroidery

Embroidery is essentially the process of stitching a design onto fabric. You can do this by hand or machine; the choice is yours. Embroidery is a simple way to jazz up an otherwise ordinary item. Just by adding a design or two to a plain tablecloth or napkins, for example, you can quickly transform them into beautiful and elegant pieces you'll treasure for years to come.

In this chapter, we'll detail both hand and machine embroidery basics. You can choose to do one or the other, or both. You might like to try working on hand embroidery while your embroidery machine is stitching out a design. You'll get twice as much work done in the same amount of time, and you'll quickly create a collection of exquisite, handmade gifts!

Machine Embroidery Tools

- ❧ *Embroidery machine* – The two types of home embroidery machines are home sewing and embroidery machines and home embroidery-only machines. Both have the capability of computerized machine embroidery, but the home embroidery-only machines are exclusively for machine embroidery; they do not sew standard stitches.
- ❧ *Embroidery designs* – Machine embroidery designs are available on several types of media: memory cards, floppy disks, and CDs. There's also a wealth of designs available on the Internet.
- ❧ *Embroidery thread* – Embroidery thread is designed to stitch at high speeds. You'll find rayon, polyester, cotton, metallic, and specialty threads.

- ❧ *Stabilizers* – Stabilizers support or even replace fabric under the stress of stitching. Choosing an appropriate stabilizer is probably the most critical component of a successful embroidery project. Always test the stitching on a sample before working on your project to ensure you have an appropriate type and amount of stabilization.
  - Tear-away stabilizers
    - Ideal for dense stitching where tearing won't distort stitches or the fabric
    - Examples: Pellon Stitch-N-Tear, Dry Cover-Up, Kleer-Fuse, Ultra Tear
  - Cut-away stabilizers
    - Ideal for delicate fabrics that might be distorted by tearing away the stabilizer

- Examples: Sulky Cut-Away Soft 'n Sheer, Pellon Sof-Stitch, Hydro-Stick Cut-Away, Sheer Stay, Mega Stay
- **Wash-away stabilizers**
  - For use on washable fabrics; easily removed by water, leaving no visible residue
  - Examples: Avalon by Madeira, S-dSV, Sulky Ultra Solvy, Clear Away, Hydro-Solve
- **Press-on stabilizers**
  - Suited for knits and loosely woven fabrics
  - Examples: Sulky Totally Stable, Firm Hold
- **Adhesive-backed stabilizers**
  - Ideal for stabilizing fabrics too small to be hooped, or when a hoop might leave an unsightly impression
  - Examples: Tear-away–Filmoplast Stic, SIA, Wash-away–S-dSV

♥ *Machine embroidery needles* – These needles feature a specially designed needle scarf and eye which virtually eliminate thread breakage when stitching dense embroidery. Insert a new needle at the beginning of each project, and replace the needle after three to four hours of stitching. Doing so is an inexpensive way of minimizing stitching problems.

Front Side

Scarf

♥ *Templates* – Templates help you place designs precisely on your projects. There are several types of templates. Some designers offer ready-made templates, but you can also make your own using a variety of techniques. For instance, print out a copy of a design from your computer, or stitch the design onto sample cloth or clear vinyl.

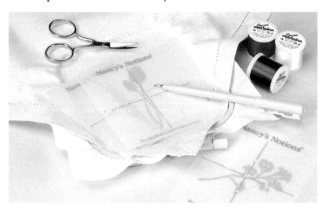

- *Prewound bobbins* – Designed specifically for machine embroidery, these bobbins tolerate the heat of high speed embroidery.

Machine Embroidery Basics

Although every brand of embroidery machine has instructions especially for that machine, some general guidelines apply to virtually every machine. Refer to these guidelines; then check your owner's manual.

1. *Optional*: Add a layer of fusible interfacing to the wrong side of the fabric before adding stabilizer(s) to add body to the fabric and prevent the stabilizer from showing through after stitching. Select a weight of interfacing similar to or lighter than the base fabric; follow the manufacturer's instructions for fusing.
2. Select a stabilizer. (See pages 88-89.)
3. Choose a design. (See page 88.)
4. Choose or create a template. (See pages 89, 93.)
5. Hoop the fabric.
   - Place the outer hoop on a flat surface. Loosen the screw.
   - Position the fabric over the hoop.

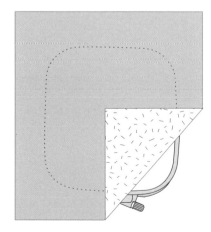

- Place the inner hoop over the fabric. Press down firmly with the heels of your hands, aligning the vertical and horizontal cross marks of the design or template with the markings on the hoop.

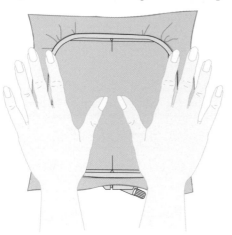

- Countersink the inner hoop, pushing it down about ⅛" for added stability. Tighten the screw.

6. Set up the machine to embroider, following your owner's manual for specific instructions.

7. Organize the thread for the design.
- Number each peg on a mini thread rack. Place the threads on the rack in the order listed on the thread sequence chart.
- If a color is used more than once, place an empty bobbin on the peg as a placeholder.

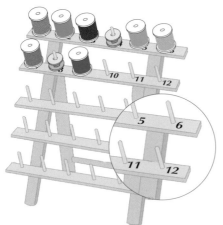

8. Stitch the design.
- Lower the presser foot. Sew a few stitches to secure the thread. Clip the thread tail.

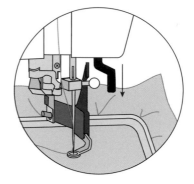

- Stitch the remainder of the first color.
- Follow the prompts on the machine that tell you when to change thread colors.
  - To change threads, raise the presser foot. Clip the needle thread at both the needle and the thread spool. Remove the thread by pulling it out through the needle. This flosses the machine tension disks and prevents lint from being drawn into the machine mechanism. It's not necessary to clip the bobbin thread.

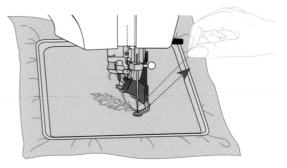

  - Thread the top of the machine with the next thread color; continue stitching.
- Repeat until all colors have been stitched.

Hand Embroidery Basics

Even if you don't own an embroidery machine, you can still enjoy making beautifully embroidered projects. Or, if you do own a machine and want something to do while your designs stitch out, give hand embroidery a try. All you need are a needle and some embroidery floss. Design options are virtually limitless and can be hand embroidered on any of the projects featured in this chapter.

1. Select a design. This can include purchased iron-on transfers, freehand drawings, traced pictures, or printouts of machine embroidery designs.
2. Trace or transfer the design onto fabric. If using an iron-on transfer, follow the manufacturer's instructions.
3. Stitch the design using the following stitches.
   - **Straight stitch** (Use three strands of embroidery floss.) Bring the needle up through the fabric at 1 and down at 2. Repeat as necessary.

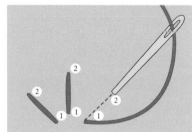

   - **French knot** (Use six strands of embroidery floss.)
     - Bring the needle up through the fabric at 1.
     - Holding the floss securely with your hand, wrap it around the needle two or three times.
     - Pulling the floss taut with your left hand, insert the needle down at 2, right next to 1.

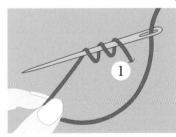

     - Pull the floss through to the back of the fabric, maintaining the tension on the floss with your left hand until the knot rests on the fabric.

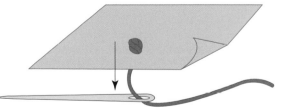

   - **Lazy daisy** (Use three strands of embroidery floss.)
     - Bring the needle up through the fabric at 1, down at 2, and up at 3, bringing the needle over the floss. Pull the floss taut.
     - Bring the needle down at 4, making a tiny stitch to anchor the loop.

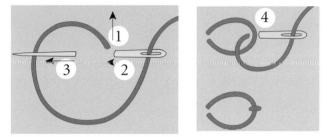

   - **Blanket stitch** (Use three strands of embroidery floss.)
     - Working from left to right, bring the needle up through the fabric at 1, down at 2, and back up at 3, bringing the needle over the floss. Pull the thread taut.

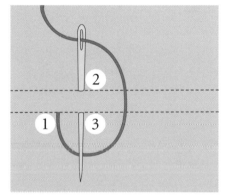

     - Repeat, working stitches evenly spaced apart.

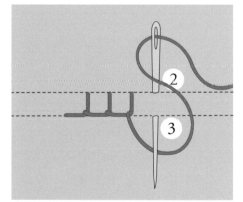

     - To make the last blanket stitch, insert the needle at 2, and pull the needle and the floss through to the back of the fabric.

Add just a touch of embroidery in the corner of a napkin and you're on your way to creating a beautiful set sure to give anyone shivers of delight. These napkins feature three different snowflake designs downloaded from the Internet. Place a single design in one corner of each napkin and make beautiful napkins that look like they were just kissed by frost. Start with purchased napkins, or quickly make your own by cutting squares of fabric and finishing the edges. Make a set of elegant napkins for every holiday and your table will always be in season!

Snow-Kissed Napkins

Materials Needed

- Set of purchased napkins
- Adhesive-backed wash-away stabilizer
- Clear vinyl

- Snowflake designs (Free on the *Sewing With Nancy* Web site, or use your favorite snowflake designs.)

Making the Napkins

1. Download the snowflake designs, following these easy steps:
   - Open your Internet connection and go to sewing-withnancy.com.

   http://www.sewingwithnancy.com

   - Click on "TV/Sewing Room."

   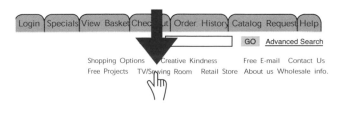

   - Click on "Free Embroidery Design – Snowflakes."

   ## TV/Sewing Room

   Sewing With Nancy® TV Shows
   Free Project Sheets
   Game Room
   Favorite Links
   Free Embroidery Design
   Free Embroidery Design—Leaf
   Free Embroidery Design—Viva La Vest Lace
   Spring Landscape Design Placement Pattern
   Free Embroidery Design—Snowflakes ◄

- Scroll down to the bottom of the page. Click on your embroidery machine format from the list below the design.
- Follow the directions to download the design to your computer's hard drive.
- Check with your machine instruction manual or dealer to determine what type of reader/writer box or software is needed to transfer the design to a memory card for that machine. (For example, you may be able to use Amazing Designs The Amazing Box or The Mini Amazing Box.)
- Follow the instructions to transfer the design to the memory card.
- Insert the memory card in the machine.

2. Create a template.
- Print out the design stored on the computer hard drive on paper, or select the appropriate type of transparency film (either ink jet or laser) for your printer.
- Mark a cross mark for the center of the design.

3. Prepare the fabric. Because the embroidered design is positioned in the corner of the napkin, use this simple hooping method.
- Starch the fabric for added stability.
- Hoop clear vinyl to serve as a stable base.
  - Cut out a window slightly larger than the design from the center of the hooped vinyl.

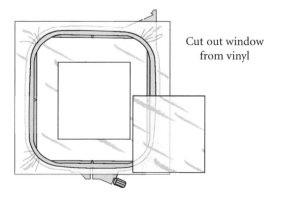

Cut out window from vinyl

- Remove the paper backing from an adhesive-backed wash-away stabilizer, and apply the adhesive stabilizer to the underside of the hooped vinyl.

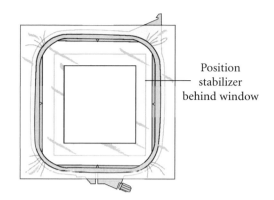

Position stabilizer behind window

- Attach the hoop to the sewing machine; center the napkin in the cut-away window.

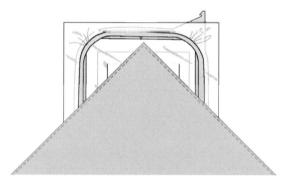

- Use a template to position a design in one corner of the napkin. Mark the starting point and/or cross marks. Remove the template. If your machine has a "trace" or "trial" function, use this to check that the design is positioned within the cut out area of the vinyl.

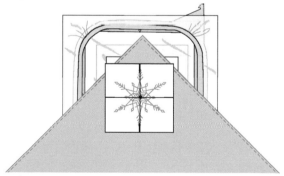

4. Stitch the design.
- Use the template to position the needle at the beginning of the snowflake; remove the template, and stitch the design.
- Cut or tear away the excess stabilizer. Rinse out the leftover bits and pieces, or just leave them in and they'll wash out the first time you launder the napkins.

Twinkle, Twinkle Little Snowflake Tablecloth

Stitch delicate snowflakes on a purchased tablecloth and create a tranquil winter scene. The scattered snowflakes suggest a gentle snowfall – you can't help but relax when you sit down at the table. This tablecloth features the same three snowflake designs used on the Snow-Kissed Napkins, pages 92-93. And since no two actual snowflakes are alike, take a hint from Mother Nature; make each of your snowflakes unique by using a different color of thread.

Materials Needed

- Purchased tablecloth
- Wash-away stabilizer
- Snowflake designs (Free on the *Sewing With Nancy* Web site, or use your favorite snowflake designs.)

Making the Tablecloth

1. Download the snowflake designs from the Internet as detailed for the napkins, pages 92-93.
2. Create templates as detailed for the napkins, page 93. For ease in planning and positioning, make the number of templates you'll need for the entire design. For instance, if you plan to stitch 10 snowflakes on your tablecloth, make 10 templates, one for each snowflake design. Then arrange all of the templates on the tablecloth for a more accurate idea of what the finished project will look like.

3. Prepare the fabric.
  - Starch the fabric for added stability.
  - Stabilize the tablecloth with an appropriate wash-away stabilizer. Follow the manufacturer's instructions for applying the stabilizer.
  - Mark the fabric for embroidery.
    - Using the templates, position the snowflakes in a scattered pattern down the center of the tablecloth, or choose another arrangement. For example, you could put the snowflakes around the border or scatter them over the entire tablecloth.
    - Mark the starting points and/or the cross marks for each design.

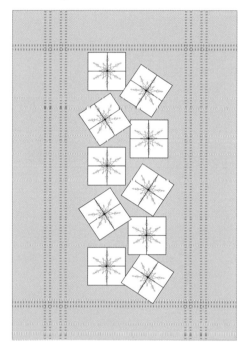

  - Hoop the stabilized fabric.

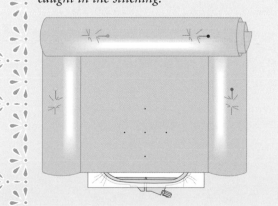

Note from Nancy

When embroidering on a large project such as a tablecloth, try rolling and pinning the fabric edges to prevent them from getting caught in the stitching.

4. Stitch the designs.
  - Use the template to position the needle at the beginning of the first snowflake; remove the template and stitch the design.

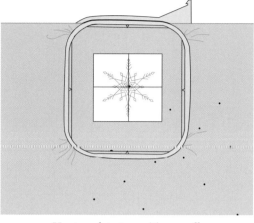

Use template to position needle

  - Position the second template over the marks; move the needle to the new starting position. (If necessary, rehoop the fabric for the second snowflake. It may be necessary to slightly loosen the hoop to accommodate the thread that has built up from the previous embroidered design.)
  - Remove the template and stitch the second snowflake.

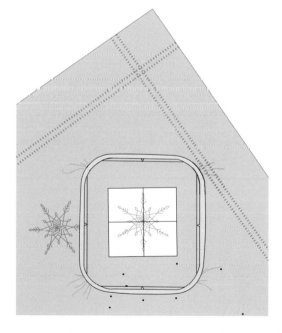

  - Repeat, using a template to position each snowflake. Stitch.
  - Cut or tear away the excess stabilizer. Rinse out the leftover bits and pieces, or just leave them in and they'll wash out the first time you launder the tablecloth.

Cast a peaceful spell on your home or winter gathering with the Peaceful Snowfall Serving Tray. An elegantly scripted message of "Peace" rests amid a background of gently falling snow. This stunning tray is perfect for serving hot, comforting drinks while sitting around the fire on snowy nights. It will transform a chilly winter evening into a relaxing retreat from the cold.

Peaceful Snowfall Serving Tray

Materials Needed   Approximate size: 12" x 16"

- Wooden serving tray with oval insert
- ½ yd. handkerchief linen
- Wash-away stabilizer
- Snowflake designs (Free on the *Sewing With Nancy* Web site, or use your favorite snowflake designs.)

- Alphabet designs (Use your machine's built-in alphabet, your favorite lettering program such as Amazing Designs Lettering Pro, or lettering designs.)

Making the Tray

1. Choose your embroidery designs.
   - Download the snowflake designs from the Internet and create templates as detailed on pages 92-93. For ease in positioning, make the number of templates you'll need for the entire design.
   - To embroider the word "Peace," refer to your embroidery machine's instruction manual to determine if your machine has a built-in alphabet. If not, or if you don't like that alphabet, use your favorite lettering program such as Amazing Designs Lettering Pro, or purchase letter designs on disk, CD, or memory card. Or, download designs from the Internet. (We used the built-in alphabet on the Baby Lock Ellagéo machine.)

2. Prepare the fabric.
   - Starch the fabric for added stability.
   - Cut a 16" x 20" rectangle of handkerchief linen. (Or cut a rectangle at least 2" larger on each side than the tray.)
   - Stabilize the fabric with an appropriate wash-away stabilizer. Follow the manufacturer's instructions for applying the stabilizer.

3. Plan the design.
   - Center the tray over the fabric. Trace around the oval opening in the tray. This is your embroidery area.

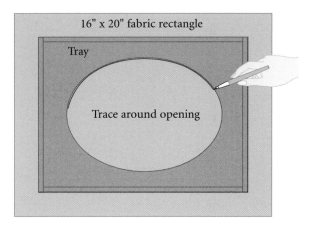

16" x 20" fabric rectangle

Tray

Trace around opening

- Use the templates to indicate the position for each design.

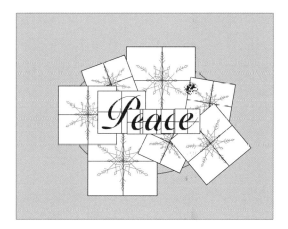

- Rotate some of the snowflakes to make them look more natural and to add variety.
- Tape the templates in place
- Mark the positions for the center and vertical and horizontal cross marks for each design.
4. Hoop the stabilized fabric.
5. Stitch the designs.
   - Stitch the background designs (the snowflakes) as detailed on page 95.

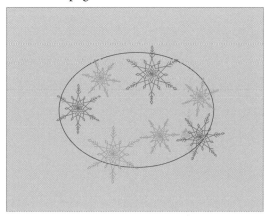

- Use the same technique to position and stitch the word "Peace."

- Remove the stabilizer.
6. Assemble the tray.
   - Loosen the screws on the tray and remove the bottom board. Remove the cardboard section.
   - Position the embroidered fabric on the cardboard section, wrapping the excess fabric around the edges.

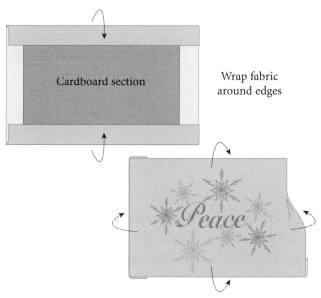

Cardboard section

Wrap fabric around edges

- Place the fabric in the oval opening, making sure the design is centered. Secure the wrapped fabric edges to the cardboard with tape or glue.
- Place the fabric in the tray, position the bottom, and screw it in place.

Frame your photos in a work of art with the Heart of Gold Picture Frame. Create the design on the frame using only two embroidery motifs and simple mirror imaging techniques. The combination of silk douppioni fabric and metallic embroidery threads catches and reflects light, adding a glowing radiance to your favorite photo. This elegant frame is an ideal project to practice mirror imaging, and it's a magnificent gift idea for anyone on your list!

Heart of Gold Picture Frame

Materials Needed Approximate size: 9" x 11¼"; photo opening: 4" x 5¼"

- ⅜ yd. Fabric A
- ⅓ yd. Fabric B
- ⅓ yd. lightweight interfacing
- Press-on cut-away stabilizer
- Adhesive-backed tear-away stabilizer

- Amazing Designer Series Hearts for All Seasons Memory Card or embroidery designs of your choice
- Hearts for All Seasons templates
- Pattern Paper
- 8½" x 11" acrylic frame
- *Optional*: Fleece batting

Making the Frame

1. Create the design pattern on paper.
   - Draw a 10" x 12¼" rectangle on Pattern Paper.
   - Measure and mark 3¼" in from each long side and 3¾" in from each short end.

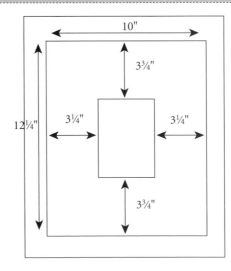

- Add ¼" seam allowances to the inner rectangle. Mark ½" from the outer rectangle to designate the embroidery area.

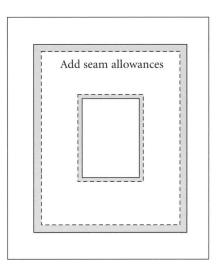

Add seam allowances

- Position the templates around the frame pattern in the desired arrangement. Mark the position of each template, noting any mirror imaging. ***Note:*** *We used designs 28670 and 28671.*

2. Cut the fabrics.
   - Fabric A:
     - Cut one 12½" x 14½" rectangle (frame front).
     - Cut one 10" x 11" rectangle (backing).
   - Fabric B: Cut one 10" x 12¼" rectangle (lining).
3. Prepare the fabric for embroidery.
   - Fuse lightweight interfacing to the wrong side of the 12½" x 14½" Fabric A rectangle.
   - Fuse the cut-away stabilizer over the interfaced side of the fabric.

- Using your paper pattern, mark the positions of the embroidery designs and the interior frame corners on the fabric. Use an air erasable marking pen and as few marks as possible to avoid damaging your fabric. (Some silk fabrics water spot.)

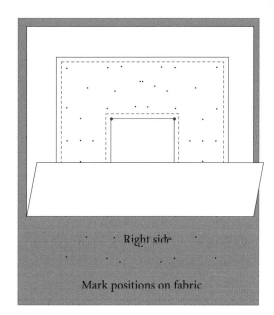

Right side

Mark positions on fabric

4. Stitch the designs using the hooping method detailed for the Snow-Kissed Napkins, page 93. Remove the excess adhesive stabilizer. Remove the cut-away stabilizer if desired.
5. Assemble the frame.
   - Allow any visible marks to disappear before pressing the embroidered fabric. Pressing over the marks sometimes makes them permanent.
   - Press from the wrong side of the fabric.

Note from Nancy

Pressing your finished embroidery designs from the wrong side avoids damaging the designs. Always place the project, embroidery side down, on a soft surface such as cotton batting before pressing.

- Place a pin straight through each interior frame corner dot and transfer the marks to the wrong side of the fabric. Draw straight guidelines connecting the dots to create a rectangle.

- Staystitch a scant ¼" from the marked rectangle toward the outer edge. Shorten the stitch length to approximately 1.5 around each corner.

- Trim each long side 3¼" wide (measure from the staystitching) and each short side 3¾" wide.

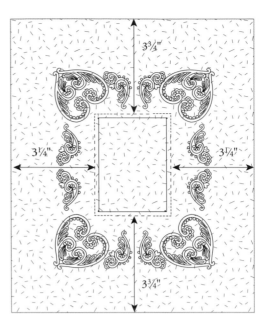

- Fuse interfacing to the wrong side of the 10" x 12¼" Fabric B rectangle.
- Position and pin the Fabric B rectangle to the embroidered Fabric A rectangle, with right sides together. Add a layer of fleece batting, if desired. Stitch the layers together, following the outside of the staystitching with a short stitch length. If the fabrics don't feed smoothly through the machine, add a light tear-away stabilizer under the batting.

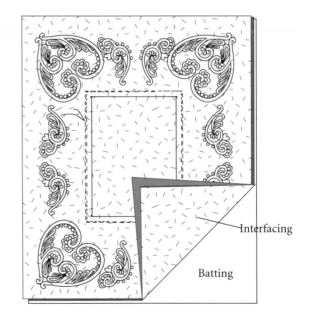

- Cut along the marked line and remove the interior rectangle. Carefully clip into each corner, right up to but not through the stitching. Press the seams flat.

Cut along marked lines, clipping into corners

- Turn the frame right side out, bringing the Fabric A rectangle through the Fabric B rectangle. Press to smooth the interior frame edges.
- If you added fleece batting, trim the batting an additional ½" on each side, being very careful not to cut the embroidered frame or the lining.
- Press under ½" seam allowances on the outer edges of the Fabric B rectangle. Press under ½" seam allowances on the embroidered Fabric A frame or, fold the frame edges over the batting and press. Pin the layers together. The finished size should be 9" x 11¼". Hand or machine sitch lower edge.

Press under ½"

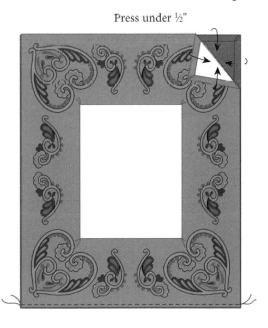

- Clean finish all the edges of the remaining Fabric A rectangle with a narrow three-thread overlock or a zigzag stitch.

- Hem one short edge. Press under ¼"; press under another ¼". Stitch.

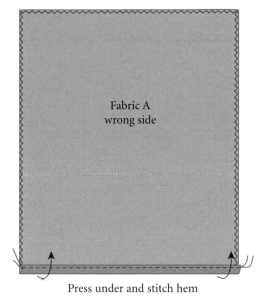

Press under and stitch hem

- Press under ½" on the remaining three sides.
- Position and pin the Fabric A backing over the Fabric B lining, meeting the pressed edges to the outer edges of the frame. Position the hemmed edge of the backing at the lower side of the embroidered frame.
- Edgestitch the layers together along the three pinned edges, ⅛" from the outer edge.

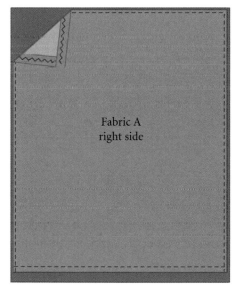

Edgestitch backing in place

6. Slip the embroidered frame over the clear acrylic frame and insert a photo. If necessary, tape the photo to the acrylic frame to keep it in place.

For a more folk art approach, try your hand at the Floral Fantasy Picture Frame. Made with felt and embellished with hand embroidery in cheery colors, this frame is sure to brighten up any room! We used the same design as the Pleased as Punch Picture Frame, page 36, to create this darling frame. It's a perfect way to showcase photos of your little sweethearts!

Floral Fantasy Picture Frame

Materials Needed Approximate size: 5¾" x 7½"; photo opening: 2" x 3¾"

- Three 6" x 7¾" felt rectangles
- Three coordinating colors of embroidery floss
- Hand sewing needle
- Water-soluble basting tape
- 5" x 7" clear acrylic frame

Making the Frame

1. Cut out the center of one 6" x 7¾" felt rectangle.
   - Measure and mark 2" in from the sides.
   - Cut along the marked lines.

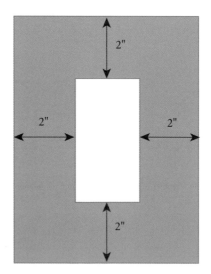

2. Transfer the design to the fabric.

- Create a template as detailed for the Pleased as Punch Picture Frame, page 36.
- Position the template over the right side of the fabric, aligning one interior corner with the mark on the template.

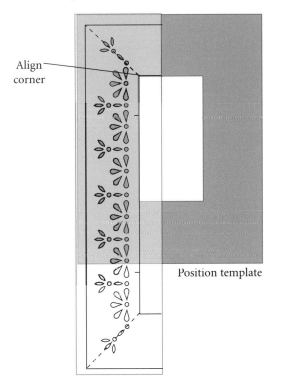

Align corner

Position template

- Mark the corners first, using an erasable fabric marking pen or pencil.

- Reposition the template and center the designs for each side.

3. Hand embroider the design using the stitches detailed on page 91.

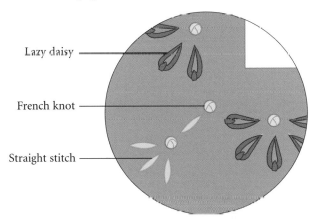

Lazy daisy

French knot

Straight stitch

4. Place the embroidered frame on a flat surface, right side up. Position the embroidered frame over a second felt rectangle, right side up. Secure the corners with very small pieces of water-soluble basting tape.

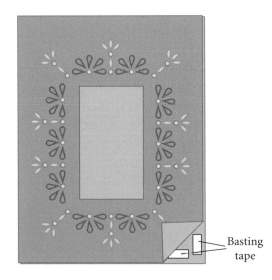

Basting tape

• Stitch around the interior rectangle, ¼" from the cut edges. Stitch across the lower edge, beginning and ending ¼" from the corners.

Stitch

• Cut out the center approximately ¼" from the stitching line. *Optional:* After cutting, use Scallop Shears to scallop the interior edges, being careful not to cut through the stitching.

Scallop edges

5. Assemble the frame.

• Position the embroidered frame front over the remaining felt rectangle with wrong sides together. If needed, secure the corners with small pieces of water-soluble basting tape.

Basting tape

• Stitch ¼" from the outer edges through all the layers of the three unstitched sides. *Optional:* Using Scallop Shears, scallop the outer edges, being careful not to cut through the stitching.

Stitch outer edges; scallop

6. Slip the felt frame over the clear acrylic frame and insert a photo. If necessary, tape the photo to the acrylic frame to keep it in place.

Turn over a new leaf with the Emerald Forest Throw Pillow. Choose two rich colors and embroider alternate squares with a leaf design. To add interest, stitch only certain colors of the design on some of the blocks. This dramatic pillow encourages daydreams of distant lands and enchanted forests.

Emerald Forest Throw Pillow

Materials Needed   Finished size: approximately 24" square

- ¾ yd. Fabric A fleece
- ½ yd. Fabric B fleece
- Adhesive-backed tear-away stabilizer
- Wash-away stabilizer

- Edge joining foot
- 18" square pillow form
- Leaf design (Free on the *Sewing With Nancy* Web site, or use your favorite leaf design.)

Making the Pillow

1. Cut the fabrics.
   - Fabric A:
     - Cut five 7" squares (pillow top).
     - Cut one 24" square (pillow back).
   - Fabric B:
     - Cut four 6" squares (pillow top).
     - Cut two 3" x 18" and two 3" x 24" strips (borders).
2. Download the leaf design from the Internet and create a template as detailed for the snowflake design, pages 92-93.

3. Hoop one Fabric A square.

Note from Nancy

Hooping a high-loft fabric such as fleece may leave an undesirable impression when the hoop is removed. To avoid the problem, try the hooping option that follows on page 106.

- Prepare the hoop.
  - Hoop an adhesive-backed tear-away stabilizer, with the paper side up.
  - Use a pin point to perforate the paper covering on the stabilizer. Remove sufficient paper to provide a sticky surface for positioning the fleece.

4. Stitch the embroidery design.

- Pick 'n Choose color options.
  - Experiment with thread colors to attain the best effect. Using a contrast color, especially for the outline, gives the greatest embroidery exposure.

- Bypass one or more of the colors in the design. Check your owner's manual to determine how to advance to the next thread color.
- Position the fabric on the sticky surface of the stabilizer.

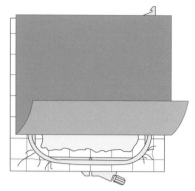

- After the design is stitched, remove the fleece from the adhesive-backed stabilizer, cutting away the design from the underside of the stabilizer, leaving the remaining stabilizer in the hoop.

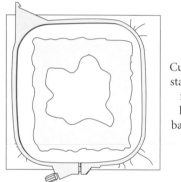

Cut away stabilizer from hoop backside

- Patch the hole in the stabilizer in the hoop by cutting a rectangle of the adhesive-backed stabilizer large enough to cover the hole. Remove the paper backing and apply the adhesive-backed stabilizer patch to the underside of the hooped stabilizer.

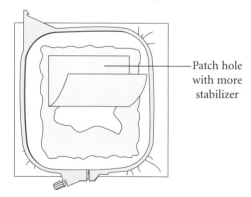

Patch hole with more stabilizer

- Position the next Fabric A square and stitch the design. Continue until all five Fabric A squares are embroidered.

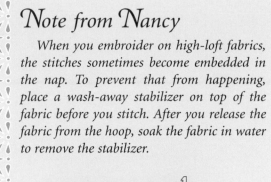

Place wash-away stabilizer over fleece

Fleece right side

5. Construct the pillow top.
- Trim the Fabric A squares to 6" square. **Note:** *During the embroidery process, the dense stitching may have pulled the fabric in toward the design. You may not have to trim much from the edges to equal 6".*
- Arrange the squares in three rows:
  - Row 1: A, B, A
  - Row 2: B, A, B
  - Row 3: A, B, A

- Join the three blocks in each row using kissed seams as detailed on page 68. Finger press the seams flat.

- Join the three rows. Finger press the seams flat.
- Attach the borders.
  - Join the 3" x 18" border strips to the top and bottom edges of the pillow top using kissed edge-joined seams.

  - Join the 3" x 24" border strips to the left and right edges of the pillow top.

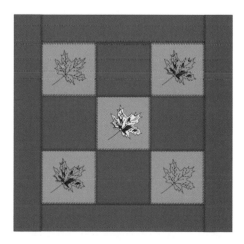

6. Assemble the pillow.

• Meet the pillow top and back, wrong sides together. Stitch around three sides using a straight stitch, sewing in the well of the seam around the pieced block.

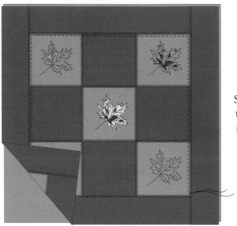

Stitch three sides

• Insert the pillow form. Stitch the fourth side closed.

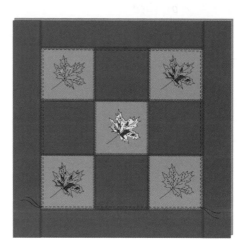

Stitch fourth side closed

Note from Nancy

For a completely different look, embroider the free leaf design on an elegant, silk evening bag. Download the leaf design as directed for the pillow. Use your favorite sizing program, such as Size Express, to reduce the design to two different sizes. Create the evening bag as detailed on pages 43-45.

Celebrate the seasons in style with these exquisite gift bags. Stitch a design on sheer organza and quickly assemble these bags. Add metallic cording and touches of metallic thread for a glistening, ethereal effect. Create bags for every occasion during the year by changing the color of organza or the design. For example, the leaf design, stitched in summery greens on white organza, is great for summer weddings. Or, change the design and use flowers. The possibilities are infinite. These bags are a delight to get – and give!

Shimmering Seasons Gift Bags

Materials Needed   Finished size: approximately 6" x 7"

- ⅜ yd. organza (makes three bags)
- Adhesive-backed wash-away stabilizer
- Reinforced Plastic
- 4½ yd. ⅛" cording
- Leaf design (Free on the *Sewing With Nancy* Web site, or use your favorite leaf design.)

Making the Bags

1. Cut the fabrics.
   - Cut three 8" x 9" organza rectangles (bag front).
   - Cut three 7" x 9" organza rectangles (bag back).
2. Download the leaf design from the Internet and create a template as detailed on pages 92-93.
3. Embroider the front of the bag.
   - Cut a piece of Reinforced Plastic larger than the hoop. This durable fabric is reinforced with a fiberglass screen. Hoop the plastic. This provides a stable base for the embroidery fabric, without actually hooping the fabric.
   - Cut a window 1" from the edges of the hoop.

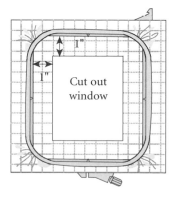

- Cut a piece of adhesive-backed wash-away stabilizer slightly larger than the window. Place the stabilizer under the window, making certain the sticky side faces upward.

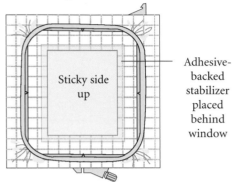

Sticky side up

Adhesive-backed stabilizer placed behind window

- Place the fabric over the sticky area. The adhesive adheres and stabilizes the fabric. Stitch the embroidery design slightly off center.

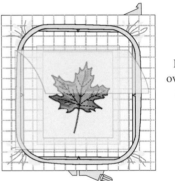

Place fabric over stabilizer; embroider

- Carefully trim away the stabilizer from the embroidery.

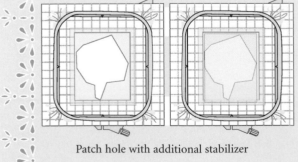
- Embroider two of the remaining organza rectangles in the same manner. (The leaf design uses multiple thread colors. Embroider each bag front varying the color order for very different colors of leaves.)
- Remove the excess wash-away stabilizer from the embroidered organza by rinsing under running water.

4. Construct the bag.
- Trim the bag front to 7" x 9".
- Meet the front and back with right sides together. Measure and mark 2½" down from the top edge on each side. Measure and mark ⅜" below the first mark.

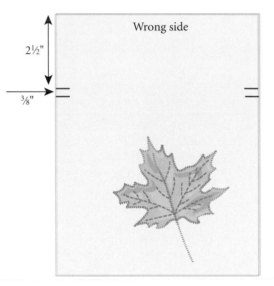

Wrong side

2½"

⅜"

- Stitch the sides with ¼" seams, leaving an opening between the two marks on each side.

Stitch sides; leave open between marks

- Fold the seams toward the center of the bag along the stitching line, wrapping the corners. Begin stitching at the fold and sew to the opposite fold. Press the seams flat.

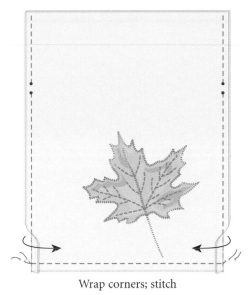

Wrap corners; stitch

- Press the seams open above the 2½" mark.
- Fold down the top edge, forming the casing. Position the raw edge ¼" below the seam openings.

Fold

¼"

- Stitch ¼" from the raw edge. Stitch again ⅜" above the first stitching line.

⅜"
¼"

Stitch

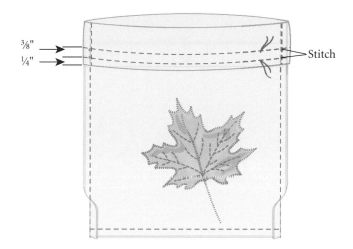

- Turn the bag right side out.
- Thread the cording through the casing.
  - Cut six 27" lengths of cording (two pieces for each bag).
  - Thread one piece of cording through the casing, entering and exiting from the same opening. Repeat on the opposite side.
  - Tie knots at the cording ends.

The weather outside may be frightful, but when you're inside creating these ornaments, everything will seem delightful. Hand embroider snowflake designs onto felt, trace and cut circles around the designs, and finish the edges. You'll create a blizzard of these cheery ornaments in no time! When the forecast calls for flurries, stay inside and enjoy the blissful warmth of the snowstorm that you create!

Blissful Blizzard Ornaments

Materials Needed   Approximate size in diameter: small, 3¼"; medium, 4"; large, 4¾"

- ¼ yd. felt
- Embroidery floss

- Hand needle
- ¼ yd. low-loft fleece batting

Making the Ornaments

1. Transfer the designs to the fabric.
   - Create the templates as detailed for the Let it Snow Snowflakes, page 93.
   - Position the template on the right side of the fabric. Trace just the design, *not* the cutting line, using an erasable fabric marking pen or pencil.

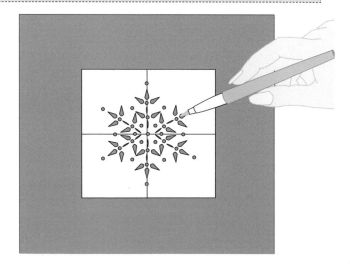

2. Hand embroider the design using the stitches detailed on page 91.

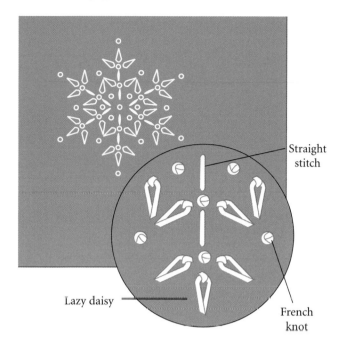

Straight stitch

Lazy daisy

French knot

3. Cut out the ornaments.
- Using a circle template or a glass, trace a circle around each snowflake, making sure the circle is at least ½" from the points of the snowflake.

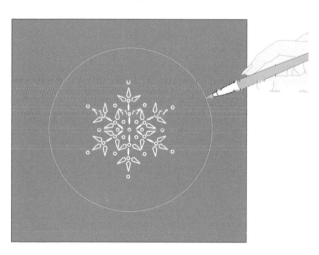

- Cut out each circle, following the traced lines. Cut a second felt circle the same size for each snowflake.
- Cut one circle of batting the same size as each ornament. Trim ¼" from the outer edges.

4. Assemble the ornaments.
- Place the plain felt circle on your work surface, wrong side up. Center a circle of batting on top. Position the embroidered snowflake on top of the batting, right side up. Pin the layers together.

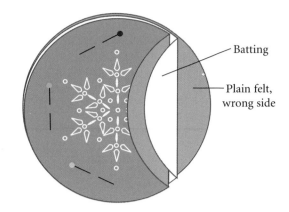

Batting

Plain felt, wrong side

- Stitch the circles together using a blanket stitch as detailed on page 91.

5. Add a hanging loop. After stitching around the circle, leave a tail of embroidery floss approximately 2" long. Braid the strands of floss together and make a hanging loop.

CHAPTER 5

Photo Transfer Treasures

*Nancy took some pictures
And picked some lovely leaves.
She created gifts so splendid
You hardly would believe!*

If your photo albums are bursting at the seams, you're running out of room for all of those frames, or you can never find fabric that's just right, then photo transfer is the technique for you! Not only is it a fun and unique way to showcase your favorite snapshots, it's also a process for making your own fabric!

Imagine creating unique projects that not only reflect the recipient's character and personal memories, but also have the potential to become treasured heirlooms, passed down for generations to come. Whether you want to preserve photos of your ancestors, capture new memories and traditions, or display collected mementos such as pressed leaves and flowers, there's a project in this chapter that is sure to catch your fancy.

Photo Transfer Basics

If you've never tried photo transfer before, you're in for a real treat! The process of transferring images to fabric is surprisingly simple. And, don't be fooled by the term "photo" transfer. You're not limited to photos. You can transfer all kinds of things – artwork, pressed flowers and leaves, ribbon, poetry, handwritten quotations, computer graphics…the list goes on and on.

Once you start experimenting with photo transfer, you'll wonder how you ever created fantastic gifts without it! Each project in this chapter provides a way of remembering those special moments from the past, whether they were 10 years or 10 minutes ago. When you give a photo transfer project as a gift, its recipient will know that it comes from the heart.

Tools

❤ *Colorfast Printer Fabric* – Print directly from a computer onto this paper-backed fabric, or use a color copier. No heat transfer or mirror imaging is required. Machine washable, it comes in 8½" x 11" sheets.

❤ *Bubble Jet Set 2000* – To make your own printer fabric, soak fabric in this clear liquid. Dry fabric remains soft with true color reproduction. One 32 oz. bottle makes about 45 sheets of printer fabric, making it an economical choice for large projects.

❤ *Southern Belle Broadcloth* – This tightly woven 200 count combed cotton fabric has a very smooth surface with minimal flecks. It's ideal for making high quality photo transfer paper.

❤ *Bubble Jet Rinse* – Use this gentle soap to machine wash your printer fabric.

❤ *Copy paper template* – This clear, acrylic template has a convenient handle and measures 8½" x 11", the perfect size for cutting photo transfer sheets for use in printers and copiers.

Transferring Images

1. Select the items you wish to transfer. In addition to color and/or black and white photos, consider:
   - Written text, such as a poem or quotation
   - Dried and pressed flowers, leaves, and other botanicals
   - Artwork (children's)
   - Bits of paper, ribbon, yarns, or silk flowers
   - Computer graphics
2. Prepare the fabric.

Using Colorfast Printer Fabric

If you like to get things done quickly and easily, then this method of photo transfer is your best bet. These printer fabric sheets are ready to use the minute you open the package. Just pop these sheets into your copier or printer, and you're on your way to fabulous projects.
   - This printer fabric doesn't require any special preparation, heat transfer, or mirror imaging.
   - Colorfast Printer Fabric has a paper backing. Be sure to print or copy onto the fabric side of the sheet.

Using Bubble Jet Set

If you plan to do a lot of photo transferring, then Bubble Jet Set is an economical choice. Start with a tight weave, high fiber count fabric such as Southern Belle Broadcloth, and actually transform it into printer fabric. Unlike many other photo transfer methods, your fabric will remain soft with true color results, making it perfect for quilts, pillows, and a host of other projects.
   - Thoroughly soak 100% cotton fabric in Bubble Jet Set for five minutes. Use any kind of container for soaking, such as a flat pan, glass casserole dish, or a bowl.
   - Let the fabric air dry. *Do not* wring the solution out of the fabric; let it drip back into the pan. Hang the fabric to dry.
   - Iron the dry sheets until they are completely smooth. Then iron them onto freezer paper, meeting the wrong side of the fabric to the shiny side of the freezer paper.
   - Trim the sheets to 8½" x 11", using the copy paper template.

3. Choose a copier or printer.
   - Copy with a color inkjet copier.
     - Load one sheet of printer fabric into the paper tray so copying occurs on the fabric side of the sheet.
     - Arrange the items on the copier glass with right sides together. ***Note:*** *If using multiple items that are layered, place the foreground elements down first and work your way to the background.*
     - Copy onto fabric. Allow sufficient time to dry.
   - Print with a color inkjet printer.
     - Load one sheet of printer fabric into the paper tray so printing occurs on the fabric side of the sheet.
     - Create an image on your computer using one of these options: Design your image on the computer screen; scan existing photos with a computer scanner; develop 35 mm film, store images on CD or floppy disk, and import them to a document; or use a digital camera and import to a document.
     - Print on the fabric side of the sheet.
4. Using the printer fabric:
   - Colorfast Printer Fabric
     - Allow the ink to dry for at least eight hours.
     - Remove the backing from the fabric. Gently rinse the fabric in cool water. Lay the fabric flat on a towel or other absorbent surface. *Do not* wring. Dry immediately. Use a hair dryer or press with a hot, dry iron.
   - Bubble Jet Set
     - Allow the ink to dry for 24 hours for best results.
     - Remove the freezer paper before using the fabric in your project.

Note from Nancy

For best results, launder your washable photo transfer projects with Bubble Jet Rinse. This mild detergent prevents color bleeding, fading, and spotting. You can also use this gentle soap to launder fabrics that are not colorfast.

Treasure the beauty of a loved one in a very special way. This quilt was created using two types of photo transfer techniques and a lot of love: the photo was transferred using a color copier, and the poem was printed from a computer. The photo and the poem blend in perfect harmony to create a lasting memory of a man's life. Hanging the quilt with a violin bow adds the perfect cadence to this tribute to a musician. This quilt is sure to become a cherished keepsake that will touch the lives and hearts of his family for years to come.

Heartstrings Memory Quilt

Materials Needed   Finished size: approximately 14½" x 21"

- ⅛ yd. Fabric A
- ⅛ yd. Fabric B
- ⅛ yd. Fabric C
- ¼ yd. Fabric D
- ⅝ yd. Fabric E (backing)
- Printer fabric
- Scraps of synthetic suede for hanging tabs

Making the Quilt

1. Transfer the photo and poem onto printer fabric as detailed on page 117.
2. Cut the fabrics.
   - Trim the photograph panel to 6¾" x 8½".
   - Trim the poem panel to 7½" x 8½".
   - Fabric A: Cut two 1¾" wide crosswise strips. Subcut into:
     - One 8½" strip (sashing)
     - Two 15" strips (framing)
     - Two 11" strips (framing)
   - Fabric B: Cut two 1½" wide crosswise strips. Subcut into:
     - Two 13" strips (inner border)
     - Two 17½" strips (inner border)
   - Fabric C: Cut two 1" wide crosswise strips. Subcut into:
     - Two 14" strips (outer border)
     - Two 19½" strips (outer border)
   - Fabric D: Cut two 2½" wide crosswise strips (binding).
   - Fabric E: Cut one 20" x 30" rectangle (backing).

3. Add the sashing, frame, and borders.
- Add the sashing strip.
  - Meet the 1¾" x 8½" Fabric A sashing strip to the right edge of the photograph panel with right sides together. Stitch, using a ½" seam.

- Repeat, adding the poem panel to the sashing strip. Press the seams toward the sashing strip.

- Add the framing strips.
  - Meet the 1¾" x 15" Fabric A framing strips to the top and bottom edges of the photo transfer panels with right sides together. Stitch.

Add horizontal framing strips

- Repeat, adding the 1¾" x 11" Fabric A framing strips to the left and right edges of the photo transfer panels.

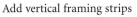

Add vertical framing strips

- Add the inner border.
  - Meet the 1½" x 17½" Fabric B inner border strips to the top and bottom edges of the framed panels with right sides together. Stitch.

- Repeat, adding the 1½" x 13" Fabric B inner border strips to the left and right edges.

- Add the outer borders.
  - Meet the 1" x 19½" Fabric C outer border strips to the top and bottom edges of the quilt with right sides together. Stitch.
  - Repeat, adding the 1" x 14" Fabric C outer border strips to the left and right edges.

4. Layer, pin, and machine quilt the quilt as detailed for the Rock-a-Bye Baby Quilt, page 53. *Optional*: After stitching in the ditch with monofilament thread, add decorative free motion quilting in the Fabric A framing using a contrasting color thread.

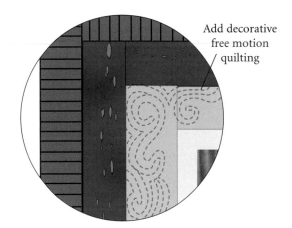

Add decorative free motion quilting

5. Complete the quilt.
   - Square up the quilt. Machine baste the edges together.
   - Add the hanging tabs.
     - Cut three 1" x 5" strips from synthetic suede.
     - Fold each strip in half, meeting the short ends.
     - Position the tabs on the upper side on the wrong side of the quilt as shown, meeting the cut edges. Baste in place. *Optional*: If you prefer to add a rod pocket, follow the instructions as detailed for the Shades of Summer Wall Hanging, page 132.

Baste tabs in place

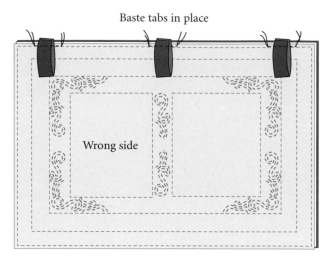

Wrong side

- Bind the quilt as detailed for the Rock-a-Bye Baby Quilt, pages 54-55. Before edgestitching the binding, fold the tabs up and pin them in place. Make sure to catch the tabs in the stitching.

Fold tabs up

Note from Nancy

To make the quilt truly special, find a unique hanger, such as a violin bow, as pictured. For instance, if the quilt is a photo of someone who loves fishing, consider using a fishing rod as a hanger. If you're displaying a photo of a gardener, use a garden hoe. Or, use knitting needles for an avid knitter. This is a great way to really personalize the quilt and to capture the spirit of the person it honors.

Who can forget their first visit to Santa Claus — the building anticipation as you wait in line to meet the jolly old elf, followed by the sheer joy of getting your turn to sit on his lap and share your Christmas wishes and dreams. With this clever pillow, you can capture those kinds of moments forever. Simply select your favorite photos from any holiday or celebration and display them on a pillowcase. It's a wonderful way to preserve and relive your family's memories all year long.

Here Comes Santa Claus Pillowcase

Materials Needed Finished size: approximately 21" x 35"

- ¾ yd. Fabric A
- ⅓ yd. Fabric B
- 2" wide crosswise strip Fabric C
- Printer fabric
- Tear-away stabilizer

Making the Pillowcase

1. Cut out the pillowcase sections.
   - Fabric A: Cut one 27" x 42" rectangle (main section).
   - Fabric B: Cut one 12" x 42" rectangle (border).
   - Fabric C: Cut one 2" x 42" strip (accent strip).
2. Construct the main section of the pillowcase as detailed for the Sweet Dreams Pillowcase, pages 23-24.
3. Create the photo transfer border.
   - Transfer the desired number of photos to printer fabric as detailed on page 117.
   - Fold the Fabric B border rectangle in half with wrong sides together, meeting the lengthwise edges. Press.

- Unfold the border. Position the photos on the right side of the fabric on one half of the border. Pin in place. If you only want photos to show on one side of the pillow, fold the border in half, meeting the short edges. Press mark the fold to provide a second positioning line.

Press mark for positioning

- Set your machine for your favorite decorative stitch. Back the fabric with a tear-away stabilizer and stitch around each photo. *Note: If you've overlapped any photos, make sure to stitch the background photo first.*

Stitch around each photo with decorative stitch

4. Add the border and accent strip to the pillowcase.
   - Fold the border strip in half with right sides together, meeting the short edges. Stitch the short edges using a ¼" seam. Press the seam open. Repeat for the accent strip.

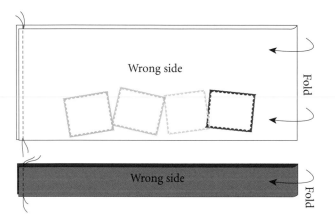

- Press the border and accent tubes in half with wrong sides together, meeting the raw edges.

- Machine baste the accent tube to the border, meeting the cut edges and matching the seamlines.

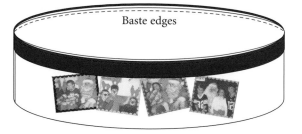

- Slip the border over the pillowcase, with the accent tube next to the right side of Fabric A, matching the seamlines. Stitch the seam.

- Serge or zigzag the raw edges. Press the seam toward the pillowcase.
- Press the accent band away from the photo transfer border.
- Topstitch the accent band close to the edge nearest the border.

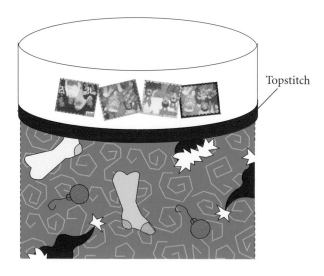

Add a personalized element to a child's playtime with the Child's Play Chalkboard Book. Use photo transfer techniques to put a child's pictures in the book, add captions and questions pertaining to each photo, and you've got an interactive activity book that's chock-full of fun! Kids will be entertained for hours reliving their favorite memories and building even more. Write on the chalkboard fabric with chalk or erasable markers, then simply wipe the pages clean, and write on them again and again. The fun never ends! A handy mesh pocket on the front cover stores chalk and/or markers. Use markers or embroidery to personalize the front cover and make the book truly unique!

Child's Play Chalkboard Book

Materials Needed   Finished size: approximately 11½" square

- ½ yd. denim
- ⅞ yd. chalkboard fabric
- ½ yd. fiberglass screen mesh fabric
- Printer fabric
- 14" zipper
- Five pkg. ½" double fold bias binding

- ¼" wide Quick Bias
- Binding and Hem Clips
- Round office-quality chalk
- Minute Miter
- Erasable markers
- Permanent fabric markers

Making the Book

1. Cut the fabrics.
   - Denim: Cut two 11½" squares (covers).
   - Chalkboard fabric: Cut eight 11½" squares ("pages").
   - Fiberglass screen mesh: Cut one 8" x 11½" rectangle (pocket).
2. Set up the sewing machine.
   - Adjust the sewing machine for a straight stitch with a stitch length of 2.5 to 3.0 (approximately 10 stitches per inch).
   - Use a size 90 needle.
   - Thread the top and bobbin of the machine with coordinating all-purpose thread. Or thread both with monofilament thread.
3. Prepare the front cover.
   - *Optional*: Personalize the front cover using one of the following options, or your favorite technique.

- Use permanent fabric markers to write the child's name and draw pictures.

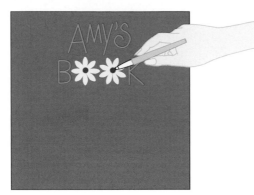

- Use machine embroidery to stitch the child's name or add designs.
- Fuse appliqué letters or designs to the cover.
• Add a pocket to the front cover.
- Center the top 11½" side of the mesh rectangle over the wrong side of the zipper, placing the mesh just below the zipper teeth. About 1" of the zipper tape will extend on each side.

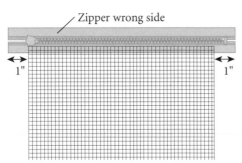

- Stitch the lower edge of the zipper tape to the mesh. Add a second row of stitching ⅛" away for reinforcement.
- Move the zipper pull tab to the center of the zipper. Trim the zipper even with the mesh.

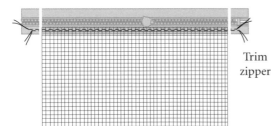

- Position the pocket on the cover, with the upper edge of the zipper tape 5" below the top edge of the cover. Align the lower edge of the pocket with the lower edge of the cover. Fold out the excess screen mesh, creating a tuck approximately ⅝" above the lower edge. Baste the screen in place along the side and lower edges.

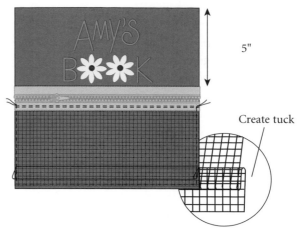

- Permanently stitch the upper edge of the zipper tape to the cover. Add a second line of stitching for reinforcement.

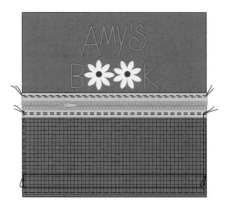

4. Transfer the photos to the printer fabric as detailed on page 117. To add text, scan the photos into your computer, or have digital camera film developed onto CD. Then print the photos and text onto the printer fabric. Trim the photos, leaving a ¼" seam allowance on all sides.

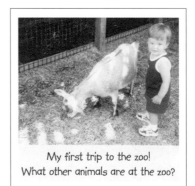

5. Prepare the chalkboard pages.
• Cure all the chalkboard squares.
- Place the fabric on a flat surface. Lay a piece of round office-quality chalk on its side on the

chalkboard surface. Rub the chalk all over the chalkboard – side to side and top to bottom. (Round the ends of the chalk so there are no sharp edges, which could permanently scratch the chalkboard fabric.)

- Clean the fabric with a damp sponge; repeat the process a second time. The chalkboard fabric squares are now "cured" and ready to use.

• Add the photos to the chalkboard pages.

- Position a photo in the corner of the chalkboard page, meeting the cut edges.

- Position ¼" wide Quick Bias along the inner edges of the photo, mitering the corner. Although heat setting is usually recommended for Quick Bias, do not use heat on chalkboard fabric because an iron will damage the fabric. Instead, finger pin the Quick Bias.

- Stitch along both edges of the Quick Bias.

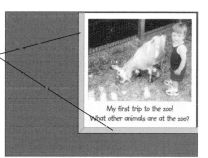

Stitch along the edges of the Quick Bias

My first trip to the zoo! What other animals are at the zoo?

- On the pages without photos, use a permanent fabric marker to draw a tic-tac-toe grid or lines to resemble a penmanship worksheet. Allow the fabric to dry flat overnight.

6. Assemble the chalkboard squares into pages.

• Place two chalkboard fabric squares with wrong sides together.

• "Pin" the layers together using Binding and Hem Clips or paper clips. Using traditional pins could leave visible nonremovable pinholes in the pages. Machine baste close to the edges to hold the layers together, removing the clips as you come to them.

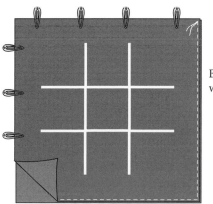

Baste edges, wrong sides together

• Repeat, creating a total of three pages.

• Back the front cover with a chalkboard fabric square with wrong sides together. Clip and baste the layers together. Repeat with the back cover.

7. Bind each layered "page" with a different color of ½" double fold bias binding.

• Starting on one edge, fold the binding in half over the edge of the chalkboard page, making sure that the bottom layer of the binding extends slightly beyond the top layer so the stitching catches both layers of the binding. Clip the binding in place.

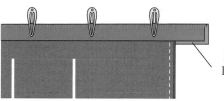

Extend bottom layer of binding slightly

• Stitch the binding in place.

- Stitch to the first corner; backstitch, stopping ⅜" from the corner with the needle down in the fabric.

- Fold the binding around the corner, overlapping the binding on the first side.

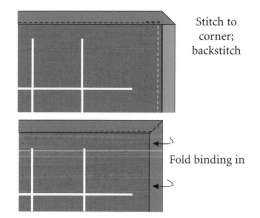

Stitch to corner; backstitch

Fold binding in

- Adjust the front and back diagonal seams so they align at the inner corner with the binding on the first side.

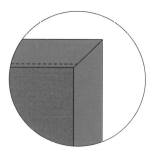

Note from Nancy

Use the Minute Miter for even easier mitering. Simply clip the Minute Miter at the corner, wrap the binding around, and gently pull up on the clip. The Minute Miter holds the binding in place until you're ready to stitch.

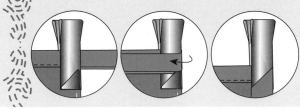

- Continue stitching, pivoting and sewing down the second side.
- Repeat, mitering each corner in this manner.
- Stop stitching 1" before the starting point.
- Cut the binding so that it extends approximately 2" past the starting point. Fold under the end of the binding.

Extend binding 2" past starting point, fold under end

- Position the binding over the starting point so that no cut edges show, and finish stitching.

8. Assemble the pages into the Chalkboard Book.
  • Create the backbone or spine for the book.
    - Cut one 12½" long piece of double fold bias binding in the color of your choice. *Optional*: Use denim, a fabric scrap, or pieced colors of leftover binding to make the spine.
    - Fold each cut end to the inside about ½" and press.
    - Fold the strip in half lengthwise; press.

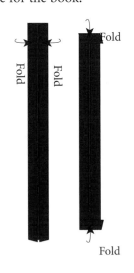

Fold

Fold

Fold

Fold

- Edgestitch through all the layers around the entire strip.

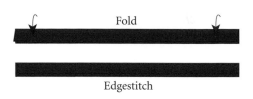

Fold

Edgestitch

• Attach the pages to the book spine.
  - Adjust the machine for a narrow blind hem stitch with a short stitch length. Starting with the back cover, chalkboard side up, position the page on the right edge of the spine. Blind hem stitch the page to the spine. The straight stitches will be on the spine, while the zigzag should catch the edge of the page.

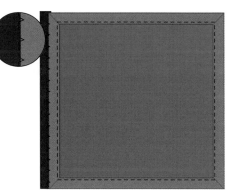

- Repeat, positioning and stitching the remaining pages to the spine one at time, aligning the upper and lower edges of the pages. Add the front cover last, placing and stitching it at the left edge of the spine.
- If you prefer hand stitching, whipstitch the pages to the book spine, starting with the back cover. Add pages one at a time, moving from the back to the front, adding the front cover last.

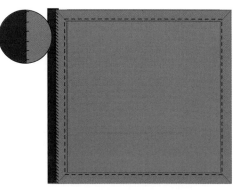

If you're running out of room on the refrigerator to display your children's and/or grandchildren's artwork, then consider these pillows instead. From coloring book to home décor, the pillow is simple to create. And kids can join in the fun, too! After coloring a picture, let them help choose fabric colors. Kids' creativity will blast off when they have the chance to display their artwork on their very own pillows!

Reach for the Stars Pillow

Materials Needed
Finished size: approximately 16" square

- ½ yd. Fabric A
- ½ yd. Fabric B
- Scraps of Fabric C for star appliqués
- Printer fabric
- Fusible interfacing

- Open toe foot
- Paper-backed fusible web
- Tear-away stabilizer
- Pillow form

Making the Pillow

1. Transfer a child's artwork to printer fabric as detailed on page 117. Trim the fabric to an 8½" square.
2. Cut the fabrics for the pillow.
   - Fabric A
     - Cut one 4½" x 8½" rectangle (border).
     - Cut one 4½" x 16½" rectangle (border).
     - Cut one 13½" x 16½" rectangle (backing).
   - Fabric B
     - Cut one 4½" x 8½" rectangle (border).
     - Cut one 4½" x 16½" rectangle (border).
     - Cut one 13½" x 16½" rectangle (backing).

3. Assemble the pillow top.

   - Meet the 4½" x 8½" Fabric A border strip to the top edge of the photo transfer rectangle, right sides together, aligning cut edges. Stitch, using a ¼" seam.
   - Repeat, stitching the 4½" x 8½" Fabric B border strip to the bottom edge of the photo transfer rectangle.
   - Press the seams toward the borders.

- Stitch the 4½" x 16½" Fabric A border strip to the left edge and the 4½" x 16½" Fabric B border strip to the right edge. Press the seams toward the borders.

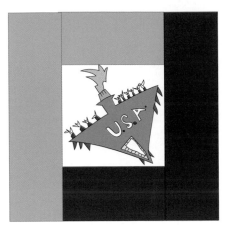

4. Add star appliqués to the pillow top.
- Trace seven stars onto the paper side of paper-backed fusible web, using the pattern on page 142. Allow approximately ¼" space around the outer edges.

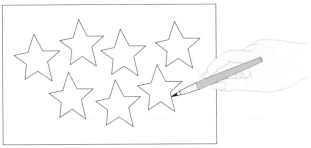

- Roughly cut out the stars, leaving ¼" margins around each design.
- Place the cut out stars on the wrong side of Fabric C, paper side up. Press.

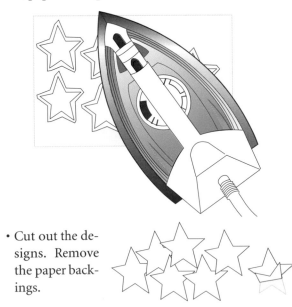

- Cut out the designs. Remove the paper backings.

- Position the stars on the Fabric A sections of the border, meeting the fusible side of the stars to the right side of the borders. Cover with a press cloth. Press.

- Set up the machine for a satin stitch.
  - Set the machine for a narrow zigzag, about 2.0 to 3.0 width and approximately 0.5 in length.
  - Insert a machine embroidery needle.
  - Thread the top of the machine with embroidery thread.
  - Use a lightweight thread such as Madeira Bobbinfil or cotton prewound bobbins in the bobbin.
  - Replace the machine's standard presser foot with an open toe foot. The opening in the front of the foot lets you see precisely where you're stitching, and a groove on the underside provides room for the stitches to easily pass under the foot.
- Back the fabric with a tear-away stabilizer.

Note from Nancy

Probably the most neglected area of working with an appliqué is the stabilizer. Make certain that you put a tear-away stabilizer underneath your fabric.

- Stitch the appliqué.
  - Satin stitch around the edges, putting a zig in the fabric and a zag in the appliqué.
  - To turn corners, stop the needle in the outside position, raise the presser foot, pivot the fabric, and continue stitching.
  - Repeat, satin stitching the six remaining stars to the pillow top.
  - Remove the stabilizer.

5. Construct the pillow back.
- Add the interfacing.
  - Cut two 4½" x 16½" rectangles from fusible interfacing.
  - Position one rectangle along one 16½" edge of the 13½" x 16½" Fabric A backing rectangle,

meeting the rough (fusible) side of the interfacing to the wrong side of the fabric.

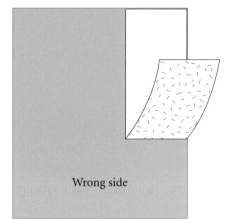

- Fuse the interfacing in place following the manufacturer's instructions. Repeat, adding interfacing to the Fabric B backing rectangle.
• Hem each backing rectangle.
- Clean finish the interfaced edge by serging or zigzagging.
- Fold under the interfaced section along the interfaced line; press. Stitch the hem in place.

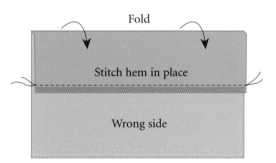

Fold

Stitch hem in place

Wrong side

• Position the Fabric A backing section over the Fabric B backing section with right sides up, aligning the rectangles to measure 16½" square. Machine baste the overlapped edges in place.

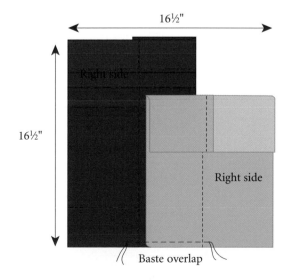

16½"

16½"

Right side

Right side

Baste overlap

6. Assemble the pillow.
• Position the pillow back over the pillow top with right sides together, aligning the edges. Pin.
• Stitch the upper and lower edges with ¼" seams.

Wrong side

• Press the seam allowances flat; then fold the seams toward the pillow center along the stitching lines and press again. This wraps the seam allowances and makes it easier to produce sharp corners and crisp edges.
• Stitch the remaining two seams, sewing from fold to fold and creating wrapped corners.
• Cut the corners at an angle.

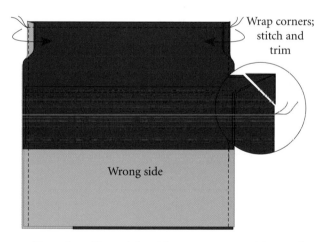

Wrap corners; stitch and trim

Wrong side

• Turn the pillow right side out, press, and insert the pillow form.
7. *Optional*: Add a back closure using buttons, hook and loop tape, or your favorite technique.

Summer is the time of year when everything seems to slow down a little. Perhaps it's the long sunny days, or the abundance of colorful flowers, urging you to kick off your shoes and take long, languid walks through the grass. There's a vibrant feeling in the air, nature is bursting with color, and everything feels alive! Capture the mood of those blissful summer days in this simple, yet elegant, wall hanging. Whether you picked some flowers during a carefree excursion or you chose some blooms from your garden, use easy photo transfer techniques to preserve those special memories in fabric and keep them blossoming for many summers to come.

Shades of Summer Wall Hanging

Materials Needed
Finished size: approximately 10¼" x 23"

- Assortment of pressed botanicals, hand-poured papers
- ⅛ yd. Fabric A
- ¼ yd. Fabric B
- ⅓ yd. Fabric C (backing)
- ⅓ yd. fleece batting
- Printer fabric

Making the Wall Hanging

1. Create the "photographic" panels.
   - Arrange dried leaves and flowers on a paper background. (We used one sheet of hand-poured paper.)
   - Transfer the arrangement to the glass bed of a color copier, with right sides to the glass. Place foreground items first, then background items. Cover the arrangement with the background paper with the right side facing the glass.
   - Copy onto printer fabric as detailed on page 117.
2. Cut the fabrics for the wall hanging.
   - Trim the photographic panels.
     - Trim two panels to 7" x 10".
     - Trim the third panel to 8" x 10".

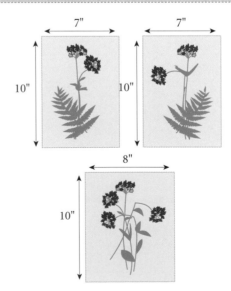

- Fabric A: Cut three 1" wide crosswise strips (flange).
- Fabric B:
  - Cut one 1½" wide crosswise strip. Subcut into two 10" long strips (sashing).
  - Cut two 2½" wide crosswise strips (binding).

3. Create the wall hanging top.
   - Add the flange accents.
     - Press each 1" wide Fabric A flange strip in half with wrong sides together, meeting the length-wise ends.

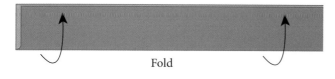

Fold

   - Meet the flange strip to the right side of one photographic panel, meeting the raw edges and starting in one corner. Machine baste the flange strip to the panel with a ¼" seam.

Stitch

   - Fold the flange strip back on itself, aligning the fold of the flange with the edge of the panel.

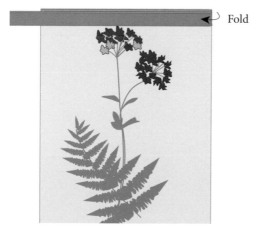

Fold

   - Fold the flange strip down, meeting the flange strip cut edge to the panel side edge, forming a miter. Machine baste the next side, starting at the cut edge.

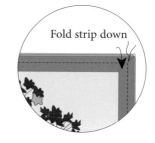

Fold strip down

   - Repeat at the remaining corners, stopping 1" before the final corner with the needle down in the fabric.
   - Fold under the flange strip, meeting the flange strip cut edges, forming a miter. Baste the remainder of the flange strip in place.

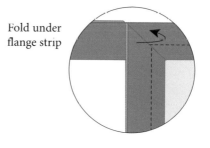

Fold under flange strip

   - Trim away the excess flange strip ends.
   - Repeat, adding a flange strip to each remaining panel.
   - Add the sashing strips.
     - Meet a Fabric B sashing strip to the right edge of one 7" x 10" panel with right sides together, sandwiching the flange strip in between. Stitch.

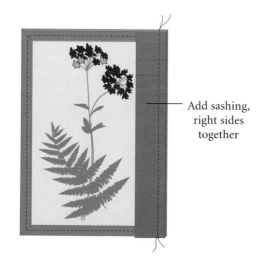

Add sashing, right sides together

- Repeat, adding the 8" x 10" panel to the sashing strip. Press the seams toward the sashing strip.

- Meet the second Fabric B sashing strip to the right edge of the 8" x 10" panel with right sides together. Stitch.

- Repeat, adding the remaining 7" x 10" panel to the sashing strip. Press the seams toward the sashing strip.

- Trim all the sashing ends even with the horizontal edges of the center panel.
4. Layer, pin, and machine quilt the wall hanging as detailed for the Rock-a-Bye Baby Quilt, page 53.
5. Complete the wall hanging.
   • Square up the wall hanging. Machine baste the edges together.
   • Add the rod pocket.
   - Cut one 3½" x 21" rectangle from the remaining backing fabric.

- Finish the 3½" edges of the rod pocket strip by zigzagging, serging, or hemming.

- Fold the strip in half with wrong sides together, meeting the lengthwise edges. Press.
- Center the rod pocket along the upper edge on the wrong side of the wall hanging, meeting the cut edges. Baste in place.

• Bind the wall hanging as detailed for the Rock-a-Bye Baby Quilt, pages 54-55.
• Roll back the folded edge of the rod pocket ¼" to ½", exposing the "back side" of the rod pocket. Finger press. Pin the finger pressed fold to the backing fabric.
• Hand stitch along the pinned fold, catching only a single layer of fabric.

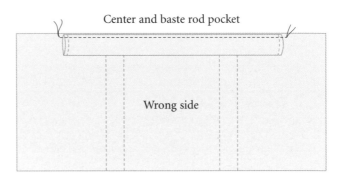

For a few months each year, the earth transforms itself into a glorious palette of rich shades of red and gold. Celebrate these exquisite colors with the Foliage Fiesta Quilted Gallery. This is the perfect excuse for taking long walks to gather leaves and foliage that you will transfer to fabric, capturing the essence of autumn forever. The gallery is as versatile as it is stunning. Use it as a table runner, or hang it on the wall either vertically or horizontally. With this quilted gallery on display all year, you can leave reality for awhile and stroll through a fantasy forest no matter what the weather is like outside.

Foliage Fiesta Quilted Gallery

Materials Needed Finished size: approximately 16" x 49"

- Printer fabric
- Assortment of pressed botanicals, hand-poured papers
- ⅝ yd. Fabric A
- ½ yd. Fabric B
- ¼ yd. Fabric C
- ¼ yd. Fabric D
- 1 yd. Fabric E (backing)
- 1 yd. fleece batting

Making the Quilted Gallery

1. Create five photographic panels as detailed for the Shades of Summer Wall Hanging, page 130.
2. Cut the fabrics for the Quilted Gallery.
   - Trim the photographic panels.
     - Trim three panels to 5" x 8" (panels 1, 3, and 5).
     - Trim two panels to 7½" x 10" (panels 2 and 4).
   - Fabric A
     - Cut one 1½" wide crosswise strip. Subcut four 5" long strips (sashing).

   - Cut one 1¾" wide crosswise strip. Subcut two 8" long strips (sashing).
   - Cut four 2" wide crosswise strips. Subcut one strip into two 15½" lengths (border).
   - Cut one 2¾" wide crosswise strip. Subcut two 7½" long strips (sashing).
   - Cut one 4¼" wide crosswise strip. Subcut into four 10" long strips (sashing).

- Fabric B
  - Cut two 1¾" wide crosswise strips. Subcut into four 7½" long strips and four 12½" long strips (sashing).
  - Cut four 2½" wide crosswise strips (binding).
- Fabric C: Cut five 1" wide crosswise strips (flange).
- Fabric D: Cut eight 1" wide crosswise strips (flange).

3. Add the flange accent strips to the photographic panels.
   - Press five 1" wide Fabric D flange strips in half with wrong sides together, meeting the lengthwise edges.

Fold

   - Add one flange strip to each photographic panel as detailed for the Shades of Summer Wall Hanging, page 131.

4. Add sashing to the photographic panels to create blocks.
   - Panels 1 and 5
     - Meet the 1½" x 5" Fabric A strips to the left and right edges of one 5" x 8" photographic panel with right sides together. Stitch, using ¼" seams. Press the seams toward the sashing.

     - Join the 4¼" x 10" Fabric A strips to the top and bottom edges.

- Panels 2 and 4
  - Join the 1¾" x 7½" Fabric B strips to the top and bottom edges of one 7½" x 10" photographic panel.
  - Join the 1¾" x 12½" Fabric B strips to the left and right edges.

- Panel 3
  - Join the 1¾" x 8" Fabric A strips to the left and right edges of one 5" x 8" photographic panel.
  - Join the 2¾" x 7½" Fabric A strips to the top and bottom edges.

5. Add the flange accent strips to the blocks.
   - Subcut two of the 1" wide Fabric C flange strips into six 12½" lengths.
   - Press the strips in half with wrong sides together, meeting the lengthwise edges.
   - Meet one flange strip to the left edge of Block 1, meeting the cut edges. Machine baste the flange strip to the block with a ¼" seam.

- Repeat, adding flange strips to the blocks as follows:
  - Block 2: Add strips to the left and right edges.
  - Block 4: Add strips to the left and right edges.
  - Block 5: Add one strip to the right edge.

6. Complete the Quilted Gallery top.
   - Meet Blocks 1 and 2 with right sides together. Stitch, using a ¼" seam.

Join blocks 1 and 2

- Repeat, joining all of the blocks.

- Add the flange accent strips.
  - Join the three remaining 1" wide Fabric C strips, seaming the strips on the diagonal to reduce bulk.
  - Press the strips in half with wrong sides together, meeting the lengthwise edges.
  - Add the flange strip to the right side of the Quilted Gallery as detailed for the Shades of Summer Wall Hanging, page 131.

Add flange strips

- Add the borders.
  - Join three 2" wide Fabric A strips, seaming the strips on the diagonal to reduce bulk.
  - Subcut the strip into two 45½" lengths.

- Join the 2" x 45½" Fabric A strips to the top and bottom edges of the Quilted Gallery. Press the seams toward the borders.

- Join the 2" x 15½" Fabric A strips to the left and right edges of the Quilted Gallery. Press the seams toward the borders.

- Add the flange accents to the borders.
  - Join the three remaining 1" wide Fabric D strips, seaming on the diagonal to reduce bulk.
  - Press the strip in half with wrong sides together, meeting the lengthwise edges.
  - Join the flange strip to the Quilted Gallery as detailed on page 131.

7. Layer, pin, machine quilt, and bind the Quilted Gallery as detailed for the Rock-a-Bye Baby Quilt, pages 53-55, using the Fabric B binding strips.

8. *Optional*: Add a rod pocket as detailed for the Shades of Summer Wall Hanging, page 132, using a 3½" x 47" rectangle of backing fabric.

Display your foliage treasures on a smaller scale in the form of a stand-up quilt. Use this as an accompaniment piece to the Quilted Gallery, or as a project on its own. If you have a large collection of pressed leaves and flowers, experiment with different fabrics and color combinations. This little quilt makes a fabulous gift for any occasion. Whether hung on a wall or displayed on an acrylic frame, it will add an elegant note to any room's décor.

Foliage Fiesta Stand-up Quilt

Materials Needed   Finished size: approximately 9½" x 11"

- ⅛ yd. Fabric A
- ¼ yd. Fabric B
- ⅛ yd. Fabric C
- ⅛ yd. Fabric D
- Printer fabric
- ⅓ yd. Fabric E (backing)
- ⅓ yd. fleece batting
- 8½" x 11" acrylic frame

Making the Quilt

1. Create one photographic panel as detailed on page 117.
2. Cut the fabrics for the quilt.
   - Trim the photographic panel to 6½" x 8".
   - Fabric A: Cut one 2" wide crosswise strip. Subcut into two 8" lengths and two 9½" lengths (borders).
   - Fabric B: Cut two 2½" wide crosswise strips (binding).
   - Fabric C: Cut two 1" wide crosswise strips (flange).
   - Fabric D: Cut one 1" wide crosswise strip (flange).
   - Fabric E: Cut two 9½" x 11" rectangles (backing and pocket).
   - Batting: Cut one 9½" x 11" rectangle.
3. Add the flange accents to the photographic panel.
   - Press the 1" wide Fabric D flange strip in half with wrong sides together, meeting the lengthwise edges.

Fold

• Add the flange strip to the panel as detailed for the Shades of Summer Wall Hanging, page 131.

4. Add the borders and outer flange accents.
  • Add the borders.
    - Meet the 2" x 8" Fabric A border strips to the left and right edges of the panel with right sides together. Stitch, using a ¼" seam. Press the seams toward the borders.

    - Repeat, adding the 2" x 9½" Fabric A border strips to the top and bottom edges.
  • Add the flange accents.
    - Join the two 1" wide Fabric C flange strips, seaming on the diagonal to reduce bulk.

    - Press the strip in half with wrong sides together, meeting the lengthwise edges.
    - Add the flange strip to the quilt as detailed for the Shades of Summer Wall Hanging, page 131.

5. Assemble the quilt.
  • Place the quilt top on your work surface, right side down. Position the batting over the rectangle. Position one 9½" x 11" Fabric E backing rectangle on top of the batting, right side up. Pin or machine baste ¼" from the cut edges.

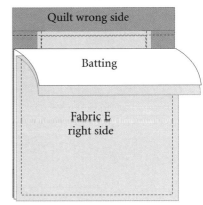

  • Add a hanging pocket.
    - Press under ½" on one short edge of the remaining 9½" x 11" Fabric E rectangle.
    - Press under another ½". Edgestitch.

    - Meet the cut edges of the pocket to the top edges of the backing. Pin or machine baste in place.

6. Bind the quilt as detailed for the Rock-a-Bye Baby Quilt, pages 54-55, using the 2½" wide Fabric B binding strips.

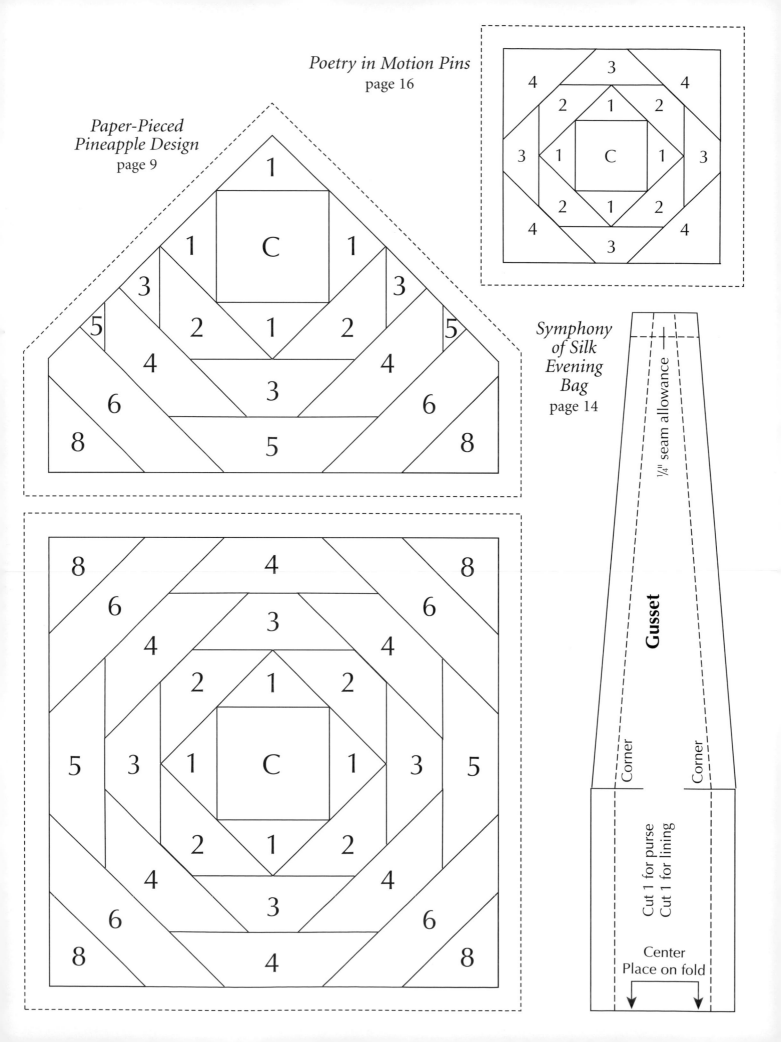

Poetry in Motion Pins
page 16

Paper-Pieced Pineapple Design
page 9

Symphony of Silk Evening Bag
page 14

¼" seam allowance

Gusset

Corner

Corner

Cut 1 for purse
Cut 1 for lining

Center
Place on fold

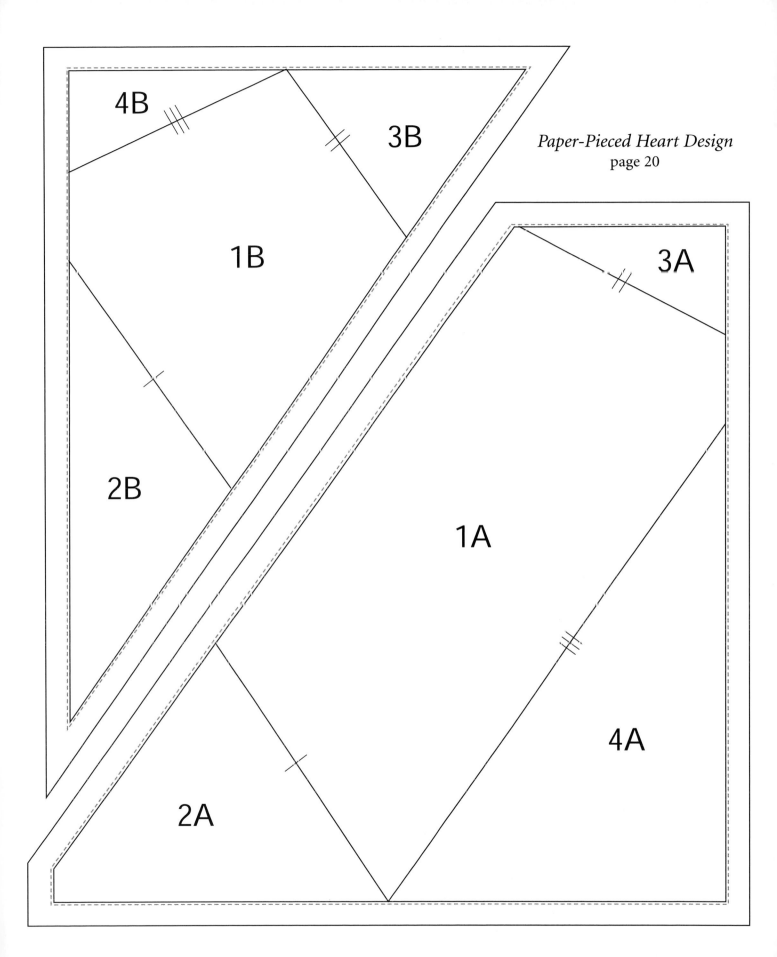

Paper-Pieced Heart Design
page 20

4B

3B

1B

3A

2B

1A

2A

4A

Eyelet-Edged Pillow
page 38

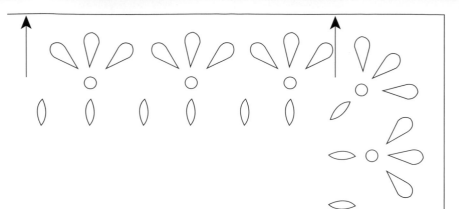

Patchwork Punch Pillow
page 40

Let it Snow Snowflakes
page 34

Pleased as Punch Picture Frame
page 36

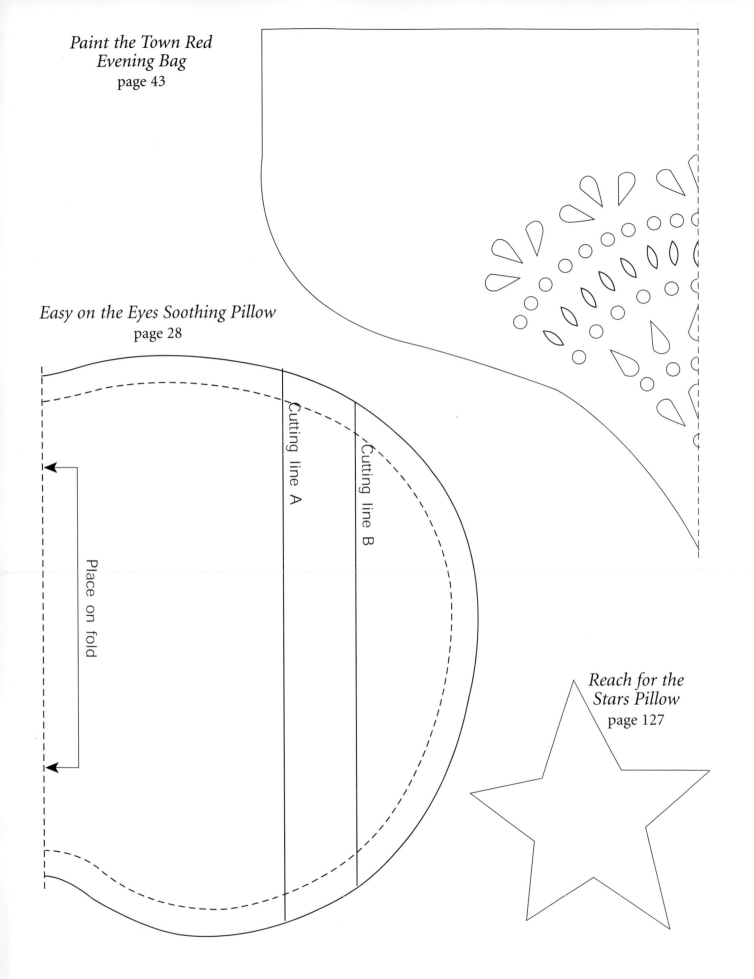

Paint the Town Red
Evening Bag
page 43

Easy on the Eyes Soothing Pillow
page 28

Cutting line A

Cutting line B

Place on fold

Reach for the
Stars Pillow
page 127

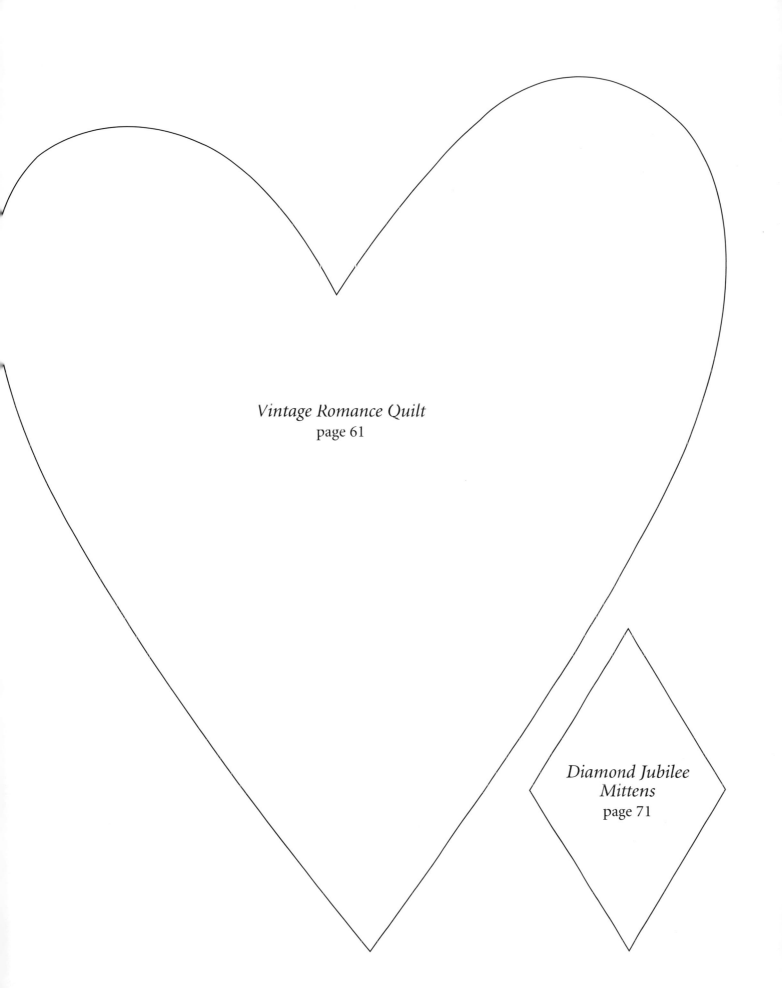

Vintage Romance Quilt
page 61

*Diamond Jubilee
Mittens*
page 71

More Creative Ideas from Nancy Zieman

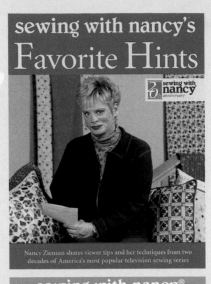

Sewing With Nancy's Favorite Hints
20th Anniversary Edition

To celebrate the 20th anniversary of her popular PBS show, Nancy Zieman brings you a collection of her favorite tips, hints, and techniques from the past two decades. You'll find tips for keeping your sewing room organized, Nancy's favorite notions, helpful sewing solutions, embroidery hints, quilting tips, and more! Relive the memories of the longest-running sewing program on public television with the nation's leading sewing authority!

Softcover • 8¼ x 10⅞ • 144 pages
Item# NFTT • $19.95

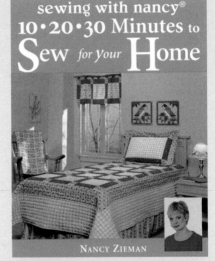

Sewing With Nancy® 10•20•30 Minutes to Sew for Your Home

This exciting new book from the host of the top-rated PBS show *Sewing With Nancy®* offers more than 25 soft-furnishing projects for every room of the home that can be completed even by those who only have 10, 20, or 30 minutes to spare. You'll quickly learn to create a quilt for the bedroom, a table runner for the kitchen, a machine mat for the sewing room, crib sheets for baby's room, and much more! Expert author Nancy Zieman's step-by-step instructions will guide you through everything from choosing fabrics and supplies to a successful finished project.

Softcover • 8¼ x 10⅞ • 96 pages
Item# MNSYH • $16.95

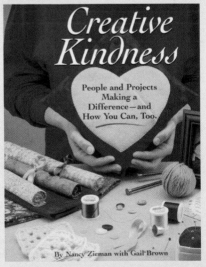

Creative Kindness
People and Projects Making a Difference – and How You Can, Too
by Nancy Zieman with Gail Brown

Make a difference in the lives of those less fortunate. Meet real life volunteers and everyday heroes as they share their stories of generosity and caring support. Create 12 projects, including a care cloth, sleepers, a sleeping bag, and pillows suitable for crafters of all skill levels by following simple step-by-step instructions. Use your sewing, quilting, knitting, and crocheting skills to help others. Experience the contagious generosity of "from hands to hearts, with hope."

Softcover • 8⅛ x 10⅞ • 96 pages
Item# CRKI • $12.99
